63

© 2021 McSweeney's Quarterly Concern and the contributors, San Francisco, California. The cover of this issue is inspired by the carvings of my grandfather Ron Lane, who was a wood sculptor in the New Forest, England. He died a few years before I was born, but I've grown up surrounded by the beautiful animals he carved. Whenever I think of any art practice, I always picture him in his studio—the careful, attentive whittling away to reveal something beautiful. When I'm working late on a comic, or when I see friends making art or writing, I think of my grandfather in his workshop—the blocks of wood stacked up by the door, waiting to be turned into animals. —*Jon McNaught, cover artist.* ASSISTED BY: Patrick Cottrell, Annie Dills, Sophia DuRose, Antonia Frydman, Sophia Frydman, Alexandra Galou, Joseph Grantham, Finn O'Neil, Matthew Petti, Selena Trager, Rachael Travers, Alvaro Villanueva, Isabella Zou. COPY EDITOR: Caitlin Van Dusen. SALES AND DISTRIBUTION MANAGER: Dan Weiss. PUBLISHING ASSOCIATE: Eric Cromie. WEB DEVELOPMENT: Brian Christian. ART DIRECTOR: Sunra Thompson. FOUNDING EDITOR: Dave Eggers. EXECUTIVE DIRECTOR: Amanda Uhle. EDITOR: Claire Boyle.

COVER ILLUSTRATIONS: Jon McNaught.

INTERIOR ILLUSTRATIONS: Arne Bellstorf.

STEPHEN DIXON PORTRAIT: Hanna Something.

MCSWEENEY'S PUBLISHING BOARD: Natasha Boas, Carol Davis, Brian Dice (president), Isabel Duffy-Pinner (secretary), Dave Eggers, Caterina Fake, Hilary Kivitz, Jordan Kurland, Nion McEvoy, Gina Pell, Jeremy Radcliffe, Jed Repko, Vendela Vida.

"Highlights and Interstices" by Jack Gilbert, originally published in *The Great Fires* (1994, Knopf), appears on page 98. Used with permission of the Jack Gilbert Estate.

Printed in Canada.

I DRINK A GLASS OF WATER:
FOUR POSTHUMOUS STORIES
BY STEPHEN DIXON

DEAR McSWEENEY'S,

Before, when I wasn't with my children, I'd feel as though I'd misplaced something. Now I'm always with my children, and I keep losing things. At a grocery store in Connecticut, near where we're holed up, I made it to the checkout counter and realized I didn't have my wallet. This place takes your temperature at the entrance, and I've been rejected before. I made eye contact with the clerk who's checked me out dozens of times. "I'm going to run and get my husband's credit card from the parking lot," I said. She nodded, smiling. She's slow and deliberate and mild. I had broken into a sweat and just resisted adding, *I'm not sick, just panicking.*

I've started burning food when I cook. At our apartment in New York City, the fire alarm is a woman's voice saying, "Fire, Fire." For a stretch, every time I turned on the stove, my daughter would ask, "Is she going to say, 'Fire, fire'?" My daughter is curious about fires. When I was little, I went to sleep making plans for fleeing a burning apartment. How would I get the cat to come with me? In Connecticut, the alarm system has a warning: "There is smoke in the house," says a woman. "The alarm will sound. The alarm is loud." My daughter asks, "Is she going to say, 'Fire, fire'?"

The line between my daughter's interest and fear is hard to gauge. She's interested in death, especially burial. When she started watching *Mister Rogers' Neighborhood*, she wanted to know whether he was alive, and then where he was buried. She wants to know where her great-grandparents are buried, and our old dogs. She wants to know if our skin is hard or soft when we die, and whether we can talk. When she asks about our bodies after death, I talk about the decomposition of a leaf. Last fall, at a coffee shop, she asked out of the blue if we could die at the same time. If not, could she hold my hand when I died? At that moment, my ex-boyfriend's brother, who lives in my neighborhood, bounded up to the table and introduced me to his wife. I was embarrassed—I had *tears* in my eyes—then grateful; he'd saved me.

Now when things get overwhelming, I turn on the TV. My son has watched *Winnie the Pooh* all the way through, once a day, for three weeks. My daughter likes *Dora the Explorer* and *Trolls*. The other morning, riding out the tail of a migraine, I tried to put on a taco documentary I'd heard about on the radio. "Will it be funny and scary?" my daughter asked, and then, after the opening credits, "So there are no dogs in this?" We lasted ten minutes before she drifted away. Later that morning, I picked a collection of Robert Aickman stories off the shelf and read: "Some people are capable of pleasure, of enjoying themselves, but none are truly capable of content."

Once, when I denied my daughter a Hershey's Kiss, she told me she was going to have me imprisoned. "Who will take care of you? Who will make you dinner?" I asked. "Papa, of course," she said. "And when he travels?" Her grandmother and babysitter could both fill in. "You know you won't get any food or water in jail," she said. "And you'll die. I'll say, *Excuse me. Is it time to bury my mother?*"

When she was a baby, my daughter bit my finger and didn't let go until I screamed. I threw her at my husband and nursed my finger while *she* screamed. Now she's five. Planning my starvation didn't make her cry. She looked at me shyly, with surprise. We were both quiet. "It's normal to want people to die," I said. "Especially your mother. I bet *Julia* wants her mom to die sometimes." I named the friend of hers I could least imagine fantasizing out loud about her mother's burial. "Really?" my daughter said. "Julia?"

In April 2020, after we'd arrived in Connecticut, my husband and I got sick. We drank hot water with ginger and took baths. One friend told me that drinking tea in the bath could "pop out" the fever. The fever popped out, and since then I've spent a lot of time preparing food. I've made madeleines, lentil fritters, meatballs, and crackers. I made whole-wheat chocolate-chip cookies that gave me and my son mild food poisoning. I felt queasy, and he puked for four hours in the middle of the night—on his bed, on my bed, on the towels we laid out after we'd stripped the sheets. We slept on a tiny, almost-clean corner of the mattress. The next day I stuffed the cookies down the garbage disposal.

My son tries everything I cook. He's two. His highest praise is "Yum." My daughter alternates between crowning me the best cook in the family and saying she wants to throw everything I've made in the garbage. If I protest, she'll sometimes say she wants to throw me in the garbage too—or that she knows I want to throw her in the garbage. "No one will ever throw you in the garbage,"

I say. "Well, why are you *looking* at me like that?" she asks.

My friend said she can't stand when writers have children and then all they write about is their children. This is hard to argue with, though I wonder how many do it purely by choice. I don't read much of that kind of work. A lot of it is close enough to my experience that I think I understand the situation and think the way the writer understands the situation is wrong. I prefer a good murder mystery.

"I'm not scared of the virus," my daughter said in February. "Did you talk about it in school?" I said. "It doesn't affect children," she told me. "You should be scared of it. Are you?"

Here's a mystery: Months ago, on the playground, a boy told my daughter he was going to kill her. "He said, 'I'm going to make you dead,'" she said. Afterward, she thought she saw the boy everywhere. He lived next door, he was in the Blue Room at her school, we passed him on the street a few times a week. "That's not him," I said. "He doesn't go to school with you. He has straight hair and that child's hair is curly. Anyway, no one is going to make you dead." When she started taking a meditation class after school, he was there too. "I don't want to go to meditation," she said. "The boy who said, 'I'm going to make you dead' is in meditation." I put aside the idea that this was the perfect situation for meditation: Isn't it said that those who give us the most trouble are our most effective teachers? I said, "The boy who said that was little and had *yellow* hair. He isn't in meditation." When I picked her up from her last meditation class, she said, "Guess what? The boy who said, 'I'm going to make you dead' is actually *kind*." Her pronunciation of *kind* lands somewhere between "kind" and "coined." "Kind?" I said. "Yes," she said. "I talked to him all day long. Actually, I don't think he's the boy who said, 'I'm going to make you dead.' But he's kind. Actually, he's my favorite person in the world."

"How many Zooms today?" my daughter asks in the morning. "Can we FaceTime Livinia? Will you text her mom and ask for her code?" FaceTimes with her friends are hard to arrange, and she has little in-the-flesh contact with them. In lieu of a social life, she spends hours on FaceTime with my mother, propping the phone against the bed as they play Family. "Mom?" my daughter will say, and if I mistakenly answer, she says, "Not you, Mama. Not *you*. Dama." In her pretend family, my daughter has a sister instead of a brother, and I've never heard her say she was going to throw her pretend mother in the trash. When my daughter tires of Family, my mother will read to her, or just stay on the phone while my daughter watches TV. Once my mother put a cartoon on her iPad and held the phone up to it so my daughter was employing three screens to watch TV. And once, with my mother on FaceTime, my daughter tied sewing thread to the piano bench and dragged it around the house. "What is this?" I said, when I felt it slip against my shin. "What are you thinking?" I shouted. "Could hurt your brother. Could hurt you. Could hurt me." From the shiny black rectangle of the phone, my mother's voice called, "It's my fault. It's my fault."

We have wasps, and over the summer, one stung me—a little sting, through my sweatshirt. "Did it really sting you?" my daughter asked, then turned back to FaceTime. "Dama," she said, "I have to tell you something. It's a very sad story."

Last fall, home sick from school, my daughter watched an animated version of *Charlotte's Web*, a truly sad story. I was making chicken soup, and she shouted, "When will the soup be ready?" every five minutes. But at one point, in the second half of the movie, she shouted, "How long do spiders live?" Google revealed that some spiders live as long as twenty-five years, but most only one or two. This was roughly our fifth attempt at *Charlotte's Web*. I'd tried to induce her to listen to the audiobook, but she either flat-out refused or fell asleep shortly after it began. She watched the entire movie and asked at the end, "Is Charlotte alive again?" "No," I said, "but her babies are." I worried I'd made a mistake: she'd think her life meant my death. But she was distracted by her dislike of the soup. "Yuck," she said. "Next time, just broth."

"Are you my *real* mother?" she says occasionally. "I think you're someone else pretending to be my mother."

My daughter's favorite question after "Where is he/she buried?" is "Did he/she have to go to the hospital?" Or "Will I have to go to the hospital?" She's either afraid of it or very interested in it. Once, she touched a pan I'd just taken out of the oven. She screamed and dropped to the floor, writhing in pain. ("What is *writhing*?" she asked later, when she heard me describe the scene.) She screamed, writhed, and soon started coughing and spitting on the floor. "No spitting!" I yelled. "There's never a good reason to spit." When she opened her hand to reveal raw skin and, in the webbing between her thumb and index finger, two pale blisters, I regretted that; there are good reasons to spit.

I read in a Kundera novel that love is a continual interrogation. In my household, we all have a lot of questions: "Do ants sleep at night?" "Can you cut up this apple for me?" "Who is putting me to sleep?" "What foods do mice like best?"

"Do you think I will have to go to the hospital?" I asked my husband every night when I was sick.

"Do you think when you die, you'll remember me?" my daughter asked recently. "Yes," I said. I was at the stove, making oatmeal. My son, at my feet, was tearing computer paper into shapes that looked like states. I tried to remember something I'd heard about the permanence of connections forged between cells. I'd found it comforting—but what was it, exactly? I turned to speak to my daughter, but she'd already left the room.

Yours,

GILLIAN LINDEN
NORFOLK, CT

DEAR McSWEENEY'S,
It's November in New York, nine months into the pandemic and four days into a contested election. As an itinerant professor-instructor-tutor (a.k.a. "writer"), I'm left with the conclusion that it's schoolkids—who can't vote, can't see their friends, and who are about to inherit the worst of the climate crisis—who have borne the worst of this mess.

I do a lot of math tutoring, and watching my students pass through a very altered version of coming-of-age ceremonies (graduation, matriculation, standardized test taking, Zoom convocations of all sorts) has me reflecting on the pomp and circumstance of seasons yore—in particular, my own rather unusual seventh-grade graduation. It is a tale of revenge and reprisal and adolescent smugness, states of mind that, once Pennsylvania has finally been called (and therefore the election), shall likely return to me with a vengeance.

It is also the story of how I know all the words to that anthem to nonsense, "Stairway to Heaven."

I went to middle school in Indiana. I want to say that education was important to my cohort, and it was, but perhaps not the way it is here in gentrified New York. In the city, I have the impression that many students are encouraged to lobotomize themselves at an early age in the name of college preparation, whereas in the Midwest our academic aspirations were more half-assed and whimsical. When we were competitive, it was for the wrong reasons (at whose house are you more likely to be able to drink in the basement?). These misdirected efforts were even more characteristic of our extracurricular pursuits. When it came time to choose a musical instrument at school, for example, I told my parents that, for no particular reason, I had become enamored of the upright bass. I was four foot five and seventy pounds with shoes on. They said no. I settled for the cello, whose case I could at least carry like a backpack with straps.

We were all of us mediocre musicians and dramatists at my school, and perhaps it was this mediocrity that drew the band and drama teachers into a special alliance. They cochaired all our performances—holiday recitals, the eighth-grade play, variety shows—and governed rehearsals with the attitude of generals staving off a mutiny. They suspected we did not respect them. And, reader, we didn't! Or at least we were distracted by more pressing matters. Also, it was impossible to fail band.

Rehearsals were rare opportunities for social mixing, a scrambling of the usual pecking order. You, an honors student (and admit it, McSweeney's, we know you were), might have had a chance to brush shoulders with real social capital. We were obsessed with seating arrangements. It was a particularly good day if you nabbed a spot in the row behind your crush.

Given the attention all this social engineering required, it was also easy to miss instructions. Such as "Next week, anyone who would like to suggest a song for graduation must bring in a CD recording. We will evaluate all suggestions and select the winner by simple majority." Who had the time, on a spring afternoon in seventh grade, to think about such things? There were math tests and AIM chats and your crush seated right there in front of you, in real life. It was late in the day, final period, and the three grilled-cheese sandwiches you'd eaten for lunch were further clouding your judgment. A rumor was making the rounds: the drama and band teachers were having an affair.

On the fateful day the song suggestions were due, all of us arrived empty-handed, save for a boy whom I'll call Giles. Giles would later be sent away to a military academy due to his enthusiasm for prescription drugs. The song he had suggested was "Stairway to Heaven," by Led Zeppelin. As the only candidate, it was immediately adopted for the graduation ceremony—a miscarriage of democracy.

The rest of us, our dignity fleetingly galvanized, protested. We pleaded (especially the honors students). The following week, we arrived with alternatives by the Beatles, Louis Armstrong, Mariah Carey. Each was met with firm refusal. "There will be no extensions!" the band teacher roared, passing around the deranged lyrics we were now obliged to commit to memory. We had missed the deadline, and now we would bear the consequences.

If there's a bustle in your hedgerow,
don't be alarmed, now.
It's just a spring clean for the May queen...

Returning to these lyrics today, I find perhaps they're more fitting than I'd once thought. It *was* May—the season of transition—and who at thirteen does not, upon contemplating one's future, feel that "ooh, it makes me wonder"?

Or perhaps these lyrics feel appropriate only now, in 2020, when nothing else makes sense. If the headlines were to announce, tomorrow, that "there's a lady who's sure all that glitters is gold and she's buying a stairway to—" Well, I suppose I wouldn't question it. Maybe she drank a bottle of bleach.

There are so many experiences lost, McSweeney's, to this awful virus, to the awful people who have presided over it, to this stunted version of life we're living. We're spending our child-hoods and our old age apart, when it strikes me that we are more in need of company than ever. Ours is a moment to mourn lost connections and lost loves, to cultivate the nobler of human feelings.

I wonder, though, what else is lost in eliding so many daily opportunities for pettiness and small-scale revenge— for the precious luxury of getting worked up over nothing: a bustle, a hedgerow, a graduation song. The world reveals itself in moronic little glimpses, after all, in moments that never seem important at the time, but which eventually ferment into, I don't know, something like wisdom? My question, McSweeney's, is what will be the cost of this past year in isolation, of having skipped over so many of *those*? And do we make up for them all at once, in 2021?

Masks on,

JESSI JEZEWSKA STEVENS
BROOKLYN, NY

MY SWEET McSWEENEY'S,
I promised to tell you the story of my tattoos, but I haven't had the time, or the desire, to be truthful. I know you know what I mean when I say "the desire." Because the desire is the desire, no matter how you look at it, and in order to talk about tattoos, the only thing you have to have is the desire.

The other day when I went to write this, the only things I could think of were questions, and I didn't want to smother you. I ask myself so many questions that it would be best not to write them down. Instead of writing them I could take four steps, open

the refrigerator, and stick my hand into a packet of chocolate truffles that I put in the fridge to harden. In all my thirty-five years, I have never had truffles. They've seemed too appetizing to me. Like something that stiffens when you stick your hand in and pick it up. My hunger is constantly opening up on me, opening up the same way an eye opens, a mouth, a drain, a urethra. It opens up on me like that, in a fairly unbearable way.

The story of my tattoos begins, if I remember correctly, in the year 2002, when I turned seventeen. I've always had friends who are older than me, and these friends have always known one or two things more than I do, at the very least. My mom, for example, is older than me, and every time we see each other she tells me: "When you were going I was already returning." It means she knows twice as much as I can know, and of course it's true. Although for some time I've been feeling that her tortilla has started to turn, so to speak. Now it's me who is coming when she is going, or is start-ing to go. So these friends of mine took me to someone who gave tattoos for a low price, with an improvised machine and some Chinese inks that were bad for the skin. My dad—a man who was also returning when I was going—told me that in getting that tattoo I had killed a million cells, minimum. His comment will be imprinted on my brain for the rest of my life. Now every time I get a tattoo, I think first that I'm a cell assassin and second about the pleasure this new drawing will bring me, a drawing that represents me, at least in that moment and the moments immediately after I get it. Later on, that affinity fluctuates. On occasion it disappears completely, leaving me with an indefinite sadness.

The year 2015 surprised me when I realized I had the same number of tattoos as I did years. I had thirty years and thirty tattoos completed. At first sight, it seemed that not one more tattoo could fit on my body. But there's always room for a few more. Skin, mysteriously, widens and lengthens. It expands like a thought or an appetite. It distorts and develops, making room for more. My friends, who are always older than me, will look at me and tell me I look like a newspaper. It is at precisely the instant they tell me this that the idea for a new tattoo takes advantage of this new space on my skin and in my thoughts, occupying not only the mind but also something more excessive called desire—which is not born in the mind, though I haven't ever figured out where exactly it is born, assuming I'm limiting myself to the space called the body. This often happens with other emotions too—emotions that are related to and are born, like desire, out of nowhere. Nevertheless, I host on my skin a few more tattoos than you can see at a glance, because a number of the first tattoos have been covered with other tattoos, not better ones but ones that are more personal and full of character.

That's the case with the tattoo that nearly fills my right arm, an arm I particularly detest for storing more fat and flaccidness than its counterpart. The tattoo in question is a bit bungled because of how I got it. The person who gave it to me didn't have the proper qualifications. The needles they used weren't even disposable. That

speck of a person recycled needles and tied them to the axle of the machine with polyester thread usually used to sew buttons. They sterilized their needles by boiling them in a rice cooker where other strange procedures were carried out, like, for example, brewing coffee or making toast with nearly rotten bread. The rice cooker was magical, in other words. Its electric current served to satisfy whatever need arose. That tattoo was my most painful yet—the one that most expanded in me something that is not appetite. The capacity of skin to endure pain is comparable only to the capacity of the mind to endure thoughts. All sorts of thoughts stalk the mind, but the mind does not give in. Instead, it continues on its path, all the while being ambushed. The same with skin: it does not give in.

The story goes on, my sweet McSweeney's, for sixteen or eighteen more years, to arrive at this year, 2020—without a doubt flawed, without a doubt chaotic and steeped in virus, clusters, little bubbles, a lack of air, an excess of air, tattoos, and love. At the time of writing this letter, the state of Georgia hasn't even assigned its electoral votes yet, and I am already thinking of the next tattoo I'll add to my skin and that it, like the forty-two before it, will be unique to me, a happy receptacle for whichever ink: Chinese, American, vegetable.

The twenty-second of September was the seventh anniversary of my getting a tattoo suitable for a person who abandons her native country. The tattoo is a line drawing of the national hero of my country, an eccentric man who wrote poems, political speeches, travel chronicles, academic essays, and translations. A man with thoughts as free as a flock of living origamis that perhaps have a missing wing, beak, or tail but that still fly for a bit before tumbling, but then catch wind and fly again like a kite with a broken string. The man in question died from a gunshot wound on the battlefield. The poems and the books, written in what little time he had, were too few. Later, the tattoo suffered parching and lymphangitis.

Its colors: pink and green. Other materials: paper, scissors, water, cotton, Vaseline, needles, tattoo machine, gloves, iron chair, wooden bed, trash can, and blood. Length of time: short. Place: a house in front of a river. Exact hour: noon.

The best thing about tattoos, my dear McSweeney's, is that they're constant, permanent. Things come and go without warning, brutal, while the tattoo remains fixed forever in the tissue that was born to host it. I know sadness has overcome me whenever one of my tattoos gets irritated. The skin swells slightly and the pores that the drawing occupies begin to burn, as if a brave ant had bitten me or a papilloma had emerged there. I don't need an alarm clock. My tattoos let me know.

Till another Sunday,

LEGNA RODRÍGUEZ IGLESIAS
MIAMI, FL

P.S. Malevich hurt less than Kandinsky.

DEAR McSWEENEY'S,
I'm writing to you from my living room, where I sit after flying in from my kitchen, following a seven-hour layover in my bedroom. The kitchen, like so many other vacation spots, is full of overpriced bananas and underrated cheese. In this year of not going anywhere, I've gotten really fixated on that Corona beer "Find Your Beach" ad, because I like the idea that I can close my eyes and find myself on a beach instead of in the apartment where I've been stuck since March. But nine months of picturing a beach without one magically appearing in front of me left me convinced that beaches can't possibly exist anymore. So I figured I might as well unload ten pounds of sand onto my bedroom floor, mount a UV lamp on the ceiling, and make do. While I wait for the dump truck to come by, I've been keeping myself busy by deciding that every vacation I've ever taken was fantastic, especially the terrible ones.

Don't you miss a good ol' terrible vacation? I do. My head dances with visions of seven-dollar airport apples purchased amid ear-splitting overhead announcements that order people who've fallen half asleep in rock-hard chairs to get their asses on that plane to Phoenix that's leaving *right now*, while the gate for my flight changes four more times. I'm dying to share an armrest with someone who's sure that for the price of their seat, they actually get a seat and a half and is crushing me with the force of cheese on a grater. I can't wait to get off the plane to discover that my car rental company is just a little too cheap to send a shuttle to the airport, so I have to walk three miles to its counter while taking in a scenic view of garbage and weeds. Please, hand me a rental car with a SERVICE NEEDED light that blinks at random and an engine that clicks like

a metronome on ketamine. I'll use it
to drive to one of those Airbnbs where
someone's nosy neighbor takes a long
look at my large, Black self and says
some shit like *Oh, you're staying with
friends? Oh, you have friends? Now I've
heard everything.*

But I don't need an airport or a
shitty rental car or racist temporary
neighbors to be happy. I'd be thrilled
to take a vacation within Los Angeles,
where I live. What I wouldn't give
to take a vacation to the Thai place
down the street that I used to go to
so often they knew me on sight. I'd
sit around breathing other people's air
while eating spring rolls and the garlic
noodles they make hot enough to blow
a hole in my chest. Or maybe I'd take a
nighttime vacation, to feel the thrill of
breaking the curfew the city imposed
last week. As a person who has not
gone out in months, I completely
understand why the coronavirus might
wait patiently to enter a club at the
dark hour of 10:01 p.m., throw back a
drink, and get busy on the dance floor.

But I know the first vacation I'll
actually take when this is over. I will
run out of toilet paper, and instead of
going online to find that online has run
out of toilet paper again, I will drive
to a store that now seems as foreign
as anywhere I've ever traveled to. The
sand will be the tan speckled tile floors,
the sun a dose of fluorescent light
beaming down from overhead. People
will wash toward and away from me in
waves instead of maintaining a space
between us equivalent to whatever we
all think six feet is. If they're wearing
masks, it will be because Mardi Gras
is happening in aisle eight. I will grab
the toilet paper while making sure to

touch as many surfaces as I can and
licking the rest. I will leave the store,
and look up at the sky, and feel very
thankful for my parking lot beach.

Yours from my bedroom beach,

KASHANA CAULEY
LOS ANGELES, CA

DEAR McSWEENEY'S,
I've moved to the mountains for a
few months to write and, it seems,
complete the transformation into my
mother. I wake at sunrise now, as she
does, write, run, meditate, and become
ecstatic upon completing small tasks
like building fires and googling images
of scat. I'm sure you know better ways
to make a fire, but please do stuff
them, because I enjoy mine. I like to
think of them as tiny beating hearts.

My little dog is with me, which
is why I've been googling scat.
Everything in these mountains wants
him dead. We walk the forest and
I envision myself punching a hawk in
the beak, kneeing a coyote in the face,
throat-jabbing a wolf, or sometimes,
beset by all three, summoning a note
whose frequency makes them flee,
makes all the mountains and pines
collapse around where I stand, clasping
my dog, quivering but safe as hell.

I've been thinking about how we
take care of one another, which is a nice
change from thinking about how we
fail to.

I spent a year and a half working
for an Upper West Side family, whose
name and business must be kept secret
for reasons I'll reveal later. My boss,
the matriarch, spent the working
day making phone deals in the room
I shared with her and her secretaries.

Upon hanging up, she'd dictate a letter summarizing the conversation to one of her secretaries, who'd type it, then email it to the caller.

My favorite day was when she'd read an article on the wonders of bananas. She wanted to tell everyone about it. All phone calls that day began, "So-and-so, when was the last time you ate a banana?" There'd be smart, effective business dealings, then more banana talk: "Just one will add a decade to your life! How many do you have in your house right now?" At the end of the conversation, she'd cry, "Eat a banana, goodbye!," then slam the phone down on—I imagined—a high-powered associate who felt confused but cared for.

On my last day, her eldest daughter ushered me into the room where the identifying objects of the business that I will not specify were stored. She asked me to promise never to write about her mother, and I agreed. I'm giving myself permission to bend that promise now, because I'm not really writing about my charming former employer; I'm writing about my friend Adina.

I've been replaying a moment from the last night we spent together, after the Center for Brooklyn History's screening of *Moonstruck*. Adina had a New York to-do list she wanted to complete before she moved to Iowa for her master's degree, and I was joining her as much as I could. We shared a love for that movie, which we knew by heart. The moment I'm thinking about happened after the showing, after we'd taken pictures of ourselves Cher-kicking an imaginary can down the street, after we realized we were on one of the most opulent streets in

Brooklyn. We peered into one brownstone's parlor to find an honest-to-god chandelier.

I said, "Enjoy your riches."

Adina laughed.

The moment I'm thinking about is the silent one, after I'd offered a thought and before Adina validated it by laughing. The remark had landed more sharply than I'd intended, and I worried she'd think I was being cruel. Adina was funny but never cruel. She could make any—literally any—line funny by delivering it an octave below her speaking range. Where had my edge even come from? I was angry she was leaving, at everyone who'd encouraged her to get a degree I didn't think she needed, at the entire state of Iowa. Imagine the anger I felt a year later, at the cancer inside her that refused to respond to chemo.

One of the reasons I loved Adina was that she not only understood *but was able to conduct* both the conversation and the conversation that is always surrounding the conversation. In the silence between the joke and the laugh, I gave her what I give almost no one: the opportunity to unmake me. She knew I was asking, *Is this anything?* by which I meant, *Am I anything?* Her laugh said, *Of course you are*. I can't think of a better way to tell you how I feel about friendship, about how crucial it is to take care of one another's unseen parts: imagination, ego, mind, self-esteem.

Adina didn't live to see her words in *McSweeney's*. Until now, I guess.

Picture us, please, Cher-kicking invisible cans down the street, yelling in blousy accents, "Enjoy your riches!" *Enjoy ya' riches!*

Back to that banana, googling scat, and punching hawks. I just now saw one soar by this giant window. Later I'll arrange then inflame a lumber heart. A friend is coming tonight; I'm making dinner. My little dog is curled under the covers behind me, in the crescent shape that means he trusts his pack. I know because I looked it up. What wouldn't I do to keep him safe?

Eat a banana, McSweeney's. Goodbye.

Kindest regards,

MARIE-HELENE BERTINO
THE CATSKILLS, NY

DEAR McSWEENEY'S,
I've been baking lately. This is an unusual development. I don't like anything that requires strict anything. I prefer the jazzy, improvisational aesthetics of throwing together a meal from whatever's in the fridge—a frittata, a stir-fry, a lasagna—and once in a blue moon following a five-hour Julia Child recipe for boeuf bourguignon, which is really more like a one-and-a-half-hour recipe with a long break while it simmers in the oven. I like flexibility, that is, and also not doing anything in the kitchen I can't do with a glass of wine in one hand. But during quarantine I've been baking. I suppose the desire has to do less with cornbread and more with alchemy.

For the first third of quarantine, I was working on a book. In order to provide a pub date that didn't feel astronomically far away, my publisher gave me an alarmingly tight deadline—May—which I coped with by locking myself in my home office at the top of January and texting all my friends to tell them I was no longer

having fun. I need to disappear in order to write, so this felt crucial. Then, about two months later, the country closed down, and no one was having fun.

Writers love to tell you about that moment of submersion, or submission, or surrender—when the work becomes bigger than you; when the text becomes the world, and you, the writer, are its lowly physical arbiter, hammering away at a keyboard, channeling glowy beams of inspiration, a fount, a vessel, et cetera. Unfortunately, it's all true. There is a kind of alchemy that happens between the brain and the blank page to render it no longer blank. Unfortunately (fortunately), that's where I went. I tunneled deep into myself, hit the back wall of my soul, blinked, and it was May. And I had finished writing.

Then, once edits had wrapped, I didn't write much of anything in the months following.

Life happened, I mean. Quarantine inched along. I learned how to change a flat tire on a bicycle and put at least a hundred miles on my 1985 Saint Tropez. I did yoga, I did at-home workouts, I got addicted to gacha gaming, I sprouted an avocado. Like rings of a tree, these phases of being have marked my quarantine.

But now it is nearly December 2020. I still feel as though summer were just yesterday. I miss that transcendent world I disappeared into then, the world of the book, which no longer belongs exclusively to me and is in fact speeding toward the world outside, of people and places, the world where I can't go.

Baking, as it turns out, is just enough of a transmutation to give me the feeling of making something: of alchemizing reactions, its own kind of transcendence. Puffs of flour, packed brown sugar, eggs—and then it becomes, somehow, breakfast.

Here's a recipe for the cornbread I've been making. It's modified from a recipe I found on Food Network.

Preheat the oven to 375 and brown some butter (more than 4 tablespoons, less than 8) in a 12-inch cast iron skillet. If you don't have a cast iron skillet and want to make muffins instead, melt the butter in the microwave and preheat your oven anyway. Mix the dry ingredients—1¼ cups stone-ground cornmeal, ¾ cups all-purpose flour, ¼ cup brown or granulated sugar, 2 teaspoons baking powder, ½ teaspoon baking soda, and 1 teaspoon salt—in a large bowl.

Then throw about a tablespoon of apple cider vinegar into 1¼ cups milk, or if you have buttermilk, just use that. During quarantine, I finally came to terms with my lactose intolerance, so I use Lactaid milk with apple cider vinegar and it comes out the same. If you've come face to face with your lactose intolerance, too, I recommend embracing it. You've suffered enough. When the milk looks bubbly, add it to the dry ingredients, then beat two eggs lightly and add them too. If you're feeling frisky, you can add a scoop of high-fat yogurt at this point, to ensure an extra-moist bread. Toss in the browned (or melted) butter, give everything a stir, and let the chemical reactions puff up the batter. Then you can add your mix-ins of choice—chunks of sharp cheddar, pickled jalapenos, canned sweet corn—and plop the batter into your hot cast iron or a greased muffin tin.

Bake for 20 to 25 minutes. Insert a fork to check for doneness.

Having lived so many lives during quarantine, I've found yet another: I've become the person who makes you read a letter in order to get the recipe. But you didn't mind, did you? You didn't even know this was going to be about cornbread. I guess it's not. It's not about anything.

Yours,

LARISSA PHAM
BROOKLYN, NY

PEONY

by ESMÉ WEIJUN WANG

THE WIND SNAPPED AND whipped as the reeds whispered. Louisa hurried onto the patio with the wooden cheese board, slipping past Mitsuki, who stood in the sliding doorway admiring the silver-sheen lake, a bottle of Bordeaux clutched in his fist. Inari was already seated at the picnic table, waiting for the other three to gather. She held her Hasselblad to her eye and scanned the shore. Louisa settled the cheeses, kissing Inari atop her blond head.

"Voilà," Louisa said with a flourish, waving her hands. "Cheeses. We have a grand assortment."

"What we have is gloom," Mitsuki said, coming all the way out of the lake house. He rounded the table, fishing a wiggly bottle opener from his pocket: a five-dollar contraption he'd gotten from the hardware store before it burned down. "The weather leaves something to be desired."

Louisa ignored him. She asked, "Where's Lucien?"

"In the bathroom." Mitsuki filched a crumb from the block of Stilton. "We'll wait for him; don't worry."

As she sat, Louisa took the oatmeal-colored throw from her own shoulders and draped it around Inari's, freckled from the long summer. Inari reflexively took one end and spread it around Louisa—squeezing her arm, kissing her ear.

"You two." Mitsuki held the bottle between his legs, slowly twisting out the cork. "You know, I never thought I would be single by the end. I always thought I'd have *someone*. Even just to be able to *choose*. Like having someone to kiss on New Year's."

No one said anything. Louisa and Inari knew of the sneaky intimacies that had occurred between Mitsuki and Lucien on the drive north to the Upper Peninsula, where the group had decided to spend their final days. It was silly, Louisa felt, that Mitsuki and Lucien even bothered to hide it, though hiding it did help to preserve the group's fragile social fabric; it would be another thing if Mitsuki's feelings for Lucien were requited. Mitsuki loved him. Lucien took advantage of that fact, which Louisa thought was cruel. But why bother arguing? There was no use in it. "Trauma fatigue" is what the discourse called it; for the last few years, the group of friends had all burned themselves out, and now here they were, at the lake house Inari's aunt and uncle had left after killing themselves the previous winter.

The house still smelled of her aunt and uncle, Inari had said when they'd arrived a few days before. She'd wandered in, the others trailing behind her—no locked doors, no locked windows—and Louisa had rushed to take Inari's hand, wanting to comfort her wife. They'd chosen rooms—Louisa and Inari, Mitsuki, Lucien, and a spot in the kitchen for two dog bowls. Kitty, Mitsuki's Australian shepherd mix, slept with him in his room and roamed the grounds; she seemed exhausted but, unlike the humans in her midst, had no reason to fake enthusiasm, and spent most of the day in bed.

Outside, Louisa, Inari, and Mitsuki drank wine from dusty glasses they'd found in the kitchen, and eventually Lucien appeared. He was six foot four and scruffy in wire-rimmed glasses, dressed in matching piped pajamas.

"Is this the party?" he asked.

They nodded. Mitsuki, sitting in the center of an otherwise empty bench, was too shy and smitten to scoot aside. Sensing this, Louisa jumped up and switched sides so that Lucien could sit with Inari. He hunched with both elbows on the table, tilting his glass so Mitsuki could pour it full.

"To friends," Lucien said.

Everyone lifted their glasses, blinking in the bitter breeze.

Inari took a sip. Louisa could see that she was careful not to touch or look at Lucien, pretending he wasn't there. Lucien was unaccustomed to being disliked and, in fact, found it as confusing as differential equations, which he'd failed in undergrad; Louisa had tutored him that summer, bringing his grade to a C. Inari's curly hair flew back. She squinted and cocked her chin, pointing it over Mitsuki's shoulder. "You can see it pretty clearly now," she said.

Mitsuki and Louisa turned. The shadow in the sky hung like a thumbprint on a poorly developed photograph.

Mitsuki turned back first. "I hate to look at it," he said.

Louisa kept staring into the heavens. If she stared long enough, a flickering, psychedelic light danced around the shape's ragged edges. She kept looking until Inari said, "Louisa, I'm *talking* to you," and then she came back down to earth.

When Louisa found Inari after washing up, she was sitting on the floor next to the bed, smoking, in an oversize T-shirt and ragged sweatpants, and Louisa's face and hands were still damp. It had been a long time since either of them had smoked, and even longer since they'd done so indoors. But why not? was the answer to any of these questions—why not, why not be terrible and ruinous to their own bodies when it would all end soon enough? Louisa sat beside Inari and extended her hand for the Parliament. They shared it in peaceable silence; Louisa remembered, by the time it was over, why she had ended the habit. Her lips felt like they were made of ash, and her breaths were shallow. Yet she accepted the next cigarette as well, ravenous for any kind of hedonism she could get.

"I feel sorry for Mitsuki," Inari said.

Louisa exhaled a long plume. "Lucien knew Mitsuki was crazy about him. Mitsuki's always been crazy about him."

"I know. It's sad, is all."

"Well, Lucien's never exactly been a careful person."

Inari said, "Mitsuki's heartbroken. It's obvious in the way he mopes around all day. And I don't like how you can just excuse Lucien like that. He's *careless*—well, it's shitty to be so careless."

"Soon," and here Louisa pressed her lips against her own bare and bony knee, "it's not going to matter anymore."

"It matters to Mitsuki," Inari said, but she didn't pursue the issue further.

By one in the morning neither of them had slept yet, though they'd fucked for hours and dozed and taken a bath together in questionable water. ("It's rust," Louisa had insisted.) Inari took a puzzle out of her suitcase and they spread the pieces on the floorboards. When the puzzle was finished, it was supposed to look like a bouquet of peonies.

"Is seven hundred and fifty pieces a lot for a puzzle?" Louisa asked.

"It's for ages eight and up," said Inari.

Louisa carefully separated the pieces of the puzzle that looked like they were from the edges. Inari tucked one knee up so Louisa could see her simple black underwear, her preferred undergarments because they could hide any stains. So many of the puzzle pieces were pink; Louisa supposed the activity was meant to be meditative, but she found it dull, if not irritating. After half an hour all she'd managed to do was pick out the unseparated pieces from the box. Pink, pink, pink.

"I think I'm actually seven," she finally said, giving up. She rocked back onto her ass against the bed.

Inari didn't stop working on the puzzle; she'd assembled one long corner with a thick edge. Nor did she look up when Louisa pulled on her puffy coat and opened the door.

The sky glittered in the darkness, and the white moon gleamed too. Louisa walked down to the lakefront in her bare feet. The lake itself was glassy, still as death. No boats tied up to any docks. No birds crying out any lonesome songs.

Louisa reached into her pocket and pulled out a sandwich bag full of her mother's ashes. She pressed her fingers into the silt and felt shards of bone.

Slowly she waded into the water. The lake was warmer than she'd expected; it felt almost like nothingness, the embrace of a blank and empty dream. She opened the sandwich bag and overturned it, dumping the contents into the water.

Mitsuki watched from the kitchen window while Louisa scattered the ashes, and he cried as her arms dropped to her sides, the ashes drifting farther and farther out. He hadn't slept well in weeks—none of them had, really—but these days his exhaustion meant that everything was making him cry.

He thought about waiting for Louisa to return and offering her comfort, but it was such a tender moment, and he feared doing the wrong thing, even if he was Louisa's oldest friend. So he took his cup of tea and returned to his room, which was the lone room on the left side of the hallway. He climbed into his creaky bed and tried to read *The Golden Bowl*, which someone had left there on an earlier escape. Louisa felt the ash and bone stick to her legs as the water swirled around her and she wanted to sob. She attempted to brush the damp ash off her calves, ultimately sinking low into the water to wash off the detritus of her dead mother, her favorite person, and when she had done her best she returned to shore.

*   *   *

Lucien cooked for everyone in the morning—he was the only one who knew, without needing to ask, how everyone liked their breakfast. ("The world may be constantly in flux," he liked to joke, "but Inari Latvala will always like her eggs over medium.") Today he wore charcoal slacks and a pink button-up under a gray cardigan, which made Louisa raise her eyebrows.

"You look nice," she said.

"Oops," he said, handing her a plate. "Accidentally broke your yolk. Sorry!"

"Jackass." Louisa began to eat before the yolk could congeal, but she snuck a look at Inari, who rolled her eyes. "It's like being color-blind," she'd once said to Louisa. "You all see something in Lucien that I can't."

"You do look nice," Mitsuki said. The wistfulness in his voice made Louisa's teeth hurt. "What's the occasion?"

Lucien laughed and took a bite off the end of a slice of bacon. "The end of the world, of course." He handed a plate to Mitsuki.

"Oh, is that today?" Mitsuki rejoined, trying to sound equally jaunty. "I had no idea."

But they all knew. They had all known for too long that the heavenly body, moniker Ludlow-1, would strike. There was nothing to be done about it. All of them had chosen to respond in different ways over the previous year, snorting drugs and weeping and trying to tie up their countless loose ends; in the end, however, they were all at the lake house, eating bacon and eggs.

A few moments later, Lucien handed a plate to Inari.

"Thank you," Inari said.

"I'm going to eat outside," Lucien said when he'd made his own plate. "It's nice out."

"I'll come with you." Mitsuki gathered his plate and utensils; Inari began to do the same, but Louisa gently rested her hand on

Inari's leg, and she stopped. The two men exited through the slid-ing-glass door. Louisa and Inari wandered to the living room, where several dirty wineglasses had already congregated. Inari reached for one of the half-empty bottles of rosé and poured it into an empty goblet.

"You're lucky that you can't see it," Louisa said, shuddering, "that you can't feel it. It's horrible when he turns his attention on you and you're just—stuck in it. Like a tractor beam."

"And you were like that?" Inari lifted the goblet to her lips.

"At one time, sure. Back in college. Not anymore, of course. But at one time, I would've—I don't know. Gutted myself for him."

"Is he handsome, or is he a tall white man?" Inari intoned. She'd put on lipstick that morning. Her hair was white-blond, and it fell in waves to her pale shoulders. She was still wearing what she'd gone to bed in: a silk slip dress the color of champagne, stolen from one of the department stores that had shut down in the final months. No one in the group had really pinched much from the shops—what was the point—but there were things some of them had really wanted before the end, and now that they could have them, why not steal? For example, Louisa was slathering her face in La Mer these days. She would be ageless now, when agelessness meant nothing. Some things did mean something still: Inari, for example. Louisa's homophobic mother had died, and then they had taken the leap.

"What do you think they're doing out there," Louisa said, gazing out the glass doors at tall, sturdy Lucien and timid Mitsuki, whose want was legible all over his face.

"Oh, you know." Inari took a gulp, and then another. "Hurting. Getting hurt."

"I see." A pause. "Nappula... thank you," Louisa said. When Inari didn't respond, she continued: "Thank you for agreeing to do this. To make this trip with them at the end. I know it wasn't—I know you would have preferred to go away, just the two of us. And it means so much to me that we did this. They're my family."

"*I'm* your family," Inari said. Her gray nail polish seemed intentionally chipped as she wrapped her fingers around her glass, draining the goblet of its delicate pink wine. She refilled it before she brought it and the bottle with her to the bedroom, dragging the hem of her slip behind her.

Need to talk, said the text from Mitsuki, which is how Louisa found herself in Mitsuki's room. Louisa had spent the previous hours trying to make it up to Inari, joking and working on the puzzle with her and rubbing her back. Now Kitty was on Mitsuki's bed, watching them with half-open eyes as she rested her head on her paws.

"It's Lucien," Mitsuki said.

"It's always Lucien, isn't it?" Louisa asked carefully, but she watched her friend's face, and he wouldn't meet her gaze. He let his dark fringe fall over his left eye, giving him a rakish look that Louisa forever wondered, tenderly, why more people didn't fall for. And now it was too late.

"Not like that," he said impatiently. "He's in love with Inari, has been for a long time. He wants to—to *do* something about it."

"Inari?" She laughed. "*My* Inari? The elegant lesbian we all know and love?"

Mitsuki smiled. "Well, when you put it like *that*."

"Yeah. You dimwit." Louisa put her hand on his shoulder; he was wearing a thin blue sweater, an explosion of nubby pills across the front. "But thank you for telling me. You're a good friend."

His smile was now a bit mournful. "I suppose I assume everyone feels the way about him that I do."

"Most people who like men do."

"I wonder," he said, "if I could've stood a chance. If we'd had more time."

The answer was *No, not really*, Louisa thought, but instead she said, "We'll never know."

The shadow of a gull sliced noiselessly across the wall. They watched it as it collided with the darkness of the floorboards, and then Louisa said, "You know, Inari and I were going to try to have a baby until all this happened."

He pulled up straighter. "Really? You never said anything."

"Because it never went anywhere. We were saving for IVF. And in the end we only had a few thousand. That shit's expensive," she finished, trying to make her words light, to make her disappointment less heavy.

Mitsuki said, "You could've asked me. I would've loaned you the money."

"That's very kind of you," Louisa replied, "but Inari would never have gone for it. She's proud. Hell, *I'm* proud. Plus you've already done so much for me."

"I would do anything for you."

She took his hand in both of hers and they sat, watching the shadows on the wall. Out of the blue, he said, "You would make such a *great* mother."

Eventually he fell asleep and she carefully tipped him backward so that he was lying in bed with his day clothes on. She stood back a few feet to watch him, and then she left.

Inari was on the floor, working on the puzzle, when Louisa came in and shut the door behind her. With alarm, Inari reached for her, seeing the look on her face, but Louisa didn't want to be touched; she was too ashamed to be looked at, so she sat a few feet away and covered her face with her hands.

"Remember when I went to Provincetown after my mother died," she said in a rush, "to visit Lucien at his fellowship?"

"Yes." Lucien had gotten a spot at a coveted seven-month fellowship for his poetry the year before.

"I stayed with him in his living quarters. I'd done it before, of course: stayed with him in different places. He was fine, kind, Lucien.

There was a party after two of the visual artists had an exhibit, and we both got drunk."

Inari said nothing. Her hands opened and closed as she waited for the inevitable.

"I said I wanted to call you and go to bed. I was sleeping on the couch in the barn where he stayed. He said he wanted to go back too. We went upstairs and he closed the door behind us. He hugged me?" She said it like a question. "And he pressed against me, but he was... aroused. Then he tried to kiss me."

"What did you do?" Inari asked.

"I pulled away. He grabbed me—hard—and tried again. He called me a—never mind. I think he was drunk. He ended up leaving bruises. I hit him and he stopped, he apologized. We both went to sleep." Louisa uncovered her face. "Neither of us mentioned it afterward. I kept thinking, What if he doesn't remember? What if he didn't mean to do it? But then just now Mitsuki..."

"What?"

"He said Lucien was interested in you, and it made me afraid. I had to say something."

Instead of speaking, Inari moved the pink puzzle pieces around, finding none that fit. Louisa crawled forward and did the same.

"Is it possible," Louisa said, "that it was an accident? That he mistook something I did?" And Inari knew that Louisa very badly wanted it to have been an accident. After all, she'd known Lucien for almost as long as she'd known Mitsuki.

"No," said Inari. "It wasn't." She looked up at Louisa. "I wish you'd told me, Lou. I wish I wasn't spending my last days on earth with that asshole."

"We could leave," Louisa said.

"You'd be willing to leave Mitsuki behind with him? No, you wouldn't, because Mitsuki's your oldest friend." She sighed. "I don't want to fight. And especially not over him."

Louisa nodded, sniffling, snapping a corner into place.

*   *   *

Dinner was stew with wine, beef, and mushrooms; the most expensive champagne they'd been able to steal; cheeses; figs and walnuts; cheesecake, baked by Lucien, cooled in the fridge. The light was generous and poured into the dining room, but no one was in the mood to eat, and the food felt like something left over from Miss Havisham's table, though everyone drank plenty, and the champagne filled their stomachs with sugar and bubbles.

"A toast to the end of the world," Lucien said.

"To the end of the world," Mitsuki echoed, and they clinked glasses.

Louisa and Inari nestled into a corner of a living room sofa, bringing a small cheese plate and a fresh bottle of Chardonnay with them. Slowly, tipping the bottle into their mouths, they became drunk, sinking into a haze as they kissed and groped, their Époisses-smeared fingers licked clean. Mitsuki suddenly bubbled out a sob and played Fiona Apple on the enormous speakers, her low croon making everything tremble; Lucien spooned stew out of the pot and directly into his mouth like a tall and handsome beast. He transitioned to straight whiskey, neat, in a tumbler he'd found on a high shelf. Inari watched him scornfully, her mouth taut as Louisa kissed her shoulder. She imagined him pressing against Louisa like he thought it was nothing, like he could take anything and it would be his.

The light dimmed and dimmed. Louisa was drunk. Inari crossed the room, leaving Louisa half dozing on the sofa. It was like a hazy dream when Inari actually did it—Louisa almost didn't see. She would have missed it entirely if Lucien hadn't screamed, high and thin like glass smashing, as Inari slid a steak knife from one of the well-made drawers and shoved it between Lucien's ribs. There was hardly any blood at first, but then Lucien, panicking, made the mistake of yanking out the knife, which had stanched the flow, and it was too late.

"It doesn't matter," Inari kept repeating as Mitsuki wailed and crouched over the bleeding man, and Louisa jumped up, running to the three of them. Lucien, curled onto his side, lay still. Louisa wondered in horror at the red splashed in waves upon Inari's clothing. They went back to their bedroom and stripped Inari of her stained silk dress, but she was bloody to the skin.

"Lock the door," Inari said.

"It's just Mitsuki out there," Louisa breathed. She was fumbling through their suitcase, trying to find clothes; there were clothes, of course. Anything would do. But nothing, nothing would do.

Inari locked the door. The light heaved into the room, marking everything, insouciant. Inari's hand left a wet print on the knob. She sat on the bed and watched Louisa throw the entire pile of clothing onto the floor. Louisa was crouching and crying with her face in her hands, and then she fell onto her ass. She blew her nose on a T-shirt. "God," she said.

"I think God has abandoned us," Inari said, and Louisa snorted, surprising them both. She cried and cried and thought of Lucien, whom she'd known since she was eighteen, whom she'd met as a college freshman at a party. He was too tall and unbearably handsome. They had talked about John Denver, their love of dogs. He had given her his number.

Louisa climbed onto the bed and Inari wrapped her long arms around her as the light outside grew larger and brighter like a blooming peony. The house shook, a door rattling on its hinges as Mitsuki tried to get in. Light slowly filled the window, a painting of forever, enveloping the room in white.

BEARS AMONG
THE LIVING

by KEVIN MOFFETT

THEY CALL OUR TOWN the City of Trees because of the trees. Along Harrison Avenue, sycamores with their tops sheared to accommodate power lines overhead. On Foothill, massive peeling eucalyptuses. On Mills, prim maidenhairs dropping their rancid berries. Our town is a page, its streets are the lines, houses are words, and the people: punctuation. Trees are just trees. We hear church bells on Sunday but never see anyone coming out or going in. The Church of Christ has a new sign in front that says HE'S STILL LISTENING, which makes me a little sad. It makes me want to say something worth listening to. Less and less, I'm in control of what I broadcast. At a park the other day I was reading on a bench while my wife pushed our son on the swings. A woman walked up to her and said, Just a heads up: There's a man reading over there on the bench and he's not with anybody. We're all keeping an eye on him. His zipper's wide open.

* * *

It was true. I mean, it's true. Lately, while walking, I'll sometimes feel a suspect breeze on my groin and look down to find my zipper open and I haven't used the bathroom in hours. Either the craftsmanship of zippers has declined or I've been neglecting to zip. A friend tells me not to worry, that it's an evolutionary adaptation, like pattern baldness or the gluey odor certain old men acquire. My friend (his name's Andrew—calling him my friend makes him sound imaginary) thinks it's a way of keeping undesirable DNA out of the gene pool. Besides, there's no law that says you have to keep your zipper up, he says.

I'd never thought there was, but he says it so defensively, as if he were dispelling a widely held opinion. Sunday mornings, we walk our dogs together, and whenever a car in a driveway is blocking part of the sidewalk, he'll kick the bumper as we walk past.

Bad car, he tells his dog.

The limits of my language, Wittgenstein said, are the limits of my town. Something to that effect. We are bisected by freeways, circled by helicopters, tilted up toward the foothills, snug in our stalls. Will we die in our beds? Will we die in our cars? Will loved ones surround us waiting for frank instructions? Our town: a blend of street noise and birdsong, a flurry of signs, an algebra problem. People call it a bedroom community, a phrase I used to repeat because it sounded kind of lurid until I finally looked up what it meant. Asleep at night, I plot and replot my jogging circuit. Seventh to Mountain, Mountain to Baseline, Baseline to Mills, Mills to Bonita... I wake up exhausted.

Mornings, when my family's still asleep, I survey my modest claim, purposeful and sincere as a lighthouse keeper. I walk Otis into the park across from our house and we watch the overtrained border collie fetch Frisbees, catching them, stacking them one by one, and then carrying them home in his mouth. You're a good boy, too, I assure

Otis, even though both of us know the only thing keeping him from sprinting toward the foothills, never to return, is the frayed orange leash clipped to his collar.

Yesterday a local man was arrested for lewd and lascivious conduct. The newspaper said that after getting a *personal body part* stuck in a park bench, he needed the help of some bystanders to free it. Such a strange euphemism: *personal body part*. Isn't every body part personal? No wonder schizophrenics think newspapers transmit coded messages: there's too much casual ambiguity. Before I learned to read, I remember seeing a grainy photograph of a teenage boy on the front page of the paper. I asked my mother what the story was about, and she skimmed it and said, He won a prize at school. For what? I asked. Her eyes were fixed on the boy's picture. For some vegetables he grew, she said finally, and folded the newspaper and tucked it under her arm, but I could still see the doomed boy peeking out, and for the first time I noticed how the seeds of future misfortune are hidden in photographs. Only in retrospect can they be detected.

I don't have all that many memories of my father. He died a few weeks before I turned eleven. I remember him sitting in a La-Z-Boy and laughing loudly at the nightly news, and feeling kind of resentful because I couldn't figure out what was so funny. I remember overhearing him say to a friend from the track: I don't like being drunk. But I do like getting drunk. I also remember trying to watch Halley's Comet with him. He woke me at three in the morning and we sat on cabana chairs in the driveway, him sipping from a tall glass of Regal Blend, trying to get drunk but not be drunk, and me shivering and anticipating the moment the comet would scream across the atmosphere, spraying shards of fire and dust and ice. The stars pulsed. An hour passed. The moon hung there, dumb as always.

He woke me again at dawn and pointed to a faint blue scribble in the sky. Barely scratched us, he said. He handed me a chunk of charcoal, freezing cold. I found this in the front yard, he told me. I held it to my nose. Charred rock, a molar plucked from the jaw of an old god. I carried it to school in the side pocket of my backpack but forgot about it until after lunch, and by then the chunk was lost, dust.

Probably just a briquette from the grill, my mother says when I call to ask her about it. She's been drinking Gallo wine again. When she's been drinking Gallo wine, she tends not to indulge my sentimentality. Your father always had an antisocial sense of humor, she says. One summer the singer Freddy Fender performed at the horse racing track he managed, and she couldn't go, but she really wanted a signed picture. Though my father didn't want to ask for one, eventually, he gave in and got one for her: *You're the Tear in My Eye. With All My Love. Freddy Fender*. Later, years after he died, she looked at it more closely and realized it was my father's handwriting. Simply to amuse himself, he'd asked Freddy Fender for the picture but not the signature.

Laughter's supposed to be shared, she says. She tells me she accidentally watched a documentary about it. It's like a universal language, she says. Even before humans could talk, we laughed; I can't remember why. Something to do with showing we mean one another no harm, or surviving danger, the overwhelming relief of it.

She tells me how on their second date, he suddenly started laughing, and when she asked what was so funny he said, Nothing. She kept pressing him and he finally told her he'd been thinking about the sun. Whose son? she asked. No, *the* sun. What about it? she said. I just realized there's an object in the sky that will blind you if you stare straight at it. And? she asked him. You don't think that's a little amusing? he said.

And that, she says, was your father. It's how she concludes every story about him: And that was your father.

What else? she says to fill the silence (when she's been drinking Gallo wine, it's difficult to get her off the phone), and she waits and I wait to see which of us knows the answer.

The summer he died is a smear of wildfires and hostile fauna. Miles north of us, the pinewoods burned, clotting the central coast of Florida with a scorched haze. My mother, sister, and I moved to a cul-de-sac of gravy-brown condos, drew straws for the smallest bedroom (I lost), sat inside awaiting instructions from the proper authorities, and watched pine ash fall and fall. Then it rained. The fires smoldered and finally went out, and I spent the summer selling off my baseball cards and hunting snakes in the palmetto scrub behind our condo. When I came home one night covered in chigger bites, my mother brushed clear nail polish over the welts and I lay shirtless and miserable as the chiggers suffocated in their hidey-holes. My body was a decoy, a trap made of meat. I scratched off the scabs of dried polish one by one. Years later someone told me chiggers don't burrow inside skin, and that the welts, which were actually full of chigger saliva, would've healed quicker if we'd left them alone. The summer he died, I watched the retired bail bondsman next door bludgeon a cottonmouth with a shovel—the snake's severed head kept snapping while its headless body slithered away, and the retired bail bondsman grinned and gestured with the shovel as if he'd orchestrated this educational display just for me.

A sign in front of the Methodist church: GOD ISN'T ANGRY. Whenever I pass it, I say it aloud, God isn't angry, adding the unspoken verdict: He's just... disappointed.

* * *

Lately I've been thinking about the ice cream man. The ice cream man, he tunnels into our town, solves our streets, turns on his music, and waits like a spider. Nothing's more inscrutable than a darkened house. Nothing except a whole street of darkened houses. Some of us sleep, some lie in bed counting their resting heart rate. Every website agrees: its rhythm is unusual. This isn't good. We like our refrigerator magnets and our dental hygienists' hairstyles to be unusual, not our resting heart rates. I remember when sleep was so easy, a nice calm pool warmed by humming turbines... now sleep is a panicked rabbit clutched tight to my chest. Just keep still and I won't hurt you, I tell my rabbit, but you can't calm the thing you're clutching. That's been true for years. If we let him, the ice cream man would notice even the faintest tremor of need and drive toward it at once. What a fireman is to a burning building, an ice cream man is to our desire for ice cream.

Coyotes eat the cats, cats eat the songbirds, songbirds eat the morning quiet. Nothing eats the coyotes. Last year some homeowner tried poisoning them but only succeeded in making them more ornery. Our coyotes are not noble mascots. They look like starved and hunted dogs.

My son plays a song that goes, *I am, I am, I am Superman, and I can do anything*, and he asks if the singer is saying *can* or *can't*. Can, I say. The chorus repeats and he asks me again and I reassure him again. He has no tolerance yet for brooding superheroes who can't do certain things. He likes Superman. He suspects he's only pretending to be scared of Kryptonite, the way he pretends to be Clark Kent. The characters in his cartoon shows never use words like *kill* or *die*. We must eliminate them! says the skeleton lord. Punish them, destroy them, vanquish them. Temporarily, of course. Even the worst villains survive into the next week, and the next. When the skeleton lord's air fleet is brought down, the sky blooms with the black parachutes of healthy skeletons. My son leans closer to the television, willing each of them safely back to their evil lair.

I was standing around with some other parents, waiting for the kids to be released from school. I miss maps, one of them said. You know, the kind you kept in the glove compartment and had to unfold, and when you were done with them you could never quite figure out how to refold them. We all remembered those. Then everyone started sharing nostalgic artifacts from childhood. I miss thinking Columbus discovered America, someone said. I miss using my mom's makeup mirror to pretend I was walking on the ceiling. I miss getting lost. I miss feeding my neighbor's dog chicken bones through the fence. I miss carrying money loose in my pocket, back when three or four dollars was so *powerful*. I miss invisible ink. I miss feeling loyal toward my breakfast cereal. I miss getting all dressed up to have my picture taken. I miss friendship bracelets, extra credit, merit badges, participation trophies. I miss being rewarded just for following along. I miss ant farms. I miss having my foot measured. I miss thinking every rabbit I saw was the Velveteen Rabbit.

I miss when my future was more interesting to me than my past, I thought. The other parents paused and looked at me, which meant I'd said it out loud as well. They waited for an explanation. The least I could do was tell them how I used to dream of being a landscape architect, as opposed to dreaming of when I used to dream of being an landscape architect. Dreaming ahead instead of dreaming behind. I kept my eyes on the sidewalk and finally said, I also miss scratch-and-sniff stickers. Sighs of relief from the other parents, robust communal nodding. It felt good to think about things you hadn't thought about in a while. Harmless, nearly forgotten things.

Some of the stickers smelled like what they were supposed to smell like and some didn't, and every time you scratched them the smell grew fainter. Remember that? You had to make sure to ration it out because the stickers wouldn't last long. It was an object lesson. Remember? Scratching and knowing that every time you scratched you were erasing the very thing you were savoring.

Where were we? That's another phrase my mother repeats when we talk on the phone. Now, where were we? As if conversation is this punishing labyrinth we're navigating together. Careful not to lose our way, careful to measure where we're going against where we've been. Oh, now I remember, she tells me. I was telling you about those sounds coming from the roof. I thought something was trying to claw its way in—turns out something was trying to claw its way *out*...

A friend gave her a book called *When Bad Things Happen to Good People* after he died. She never read it. She put it on the only bookshelf in our house, which happened to be in my bedroom, next to the only other book we owned: *The Good Earth* by Pearl S. Buck. I must've scanned its title a thousand times before falling asleep. As a kid I imagined it as a jingle: *Bad things happen to good people in monsoons, hot-air balloons. Ancient tombs, hospital rooms*. Another friend came to the house during the funeral and took away all my father's clothes, donated them to the Salvation Army. She thought she was doing us a favor, scrubbing our closet of unwanted reminders. Years later we'd still see his golf shirts all around town. On a man pumping gas into a motorcycle. On a supermarket bag boy. Another friend leaned in close to her after the service and whispered, They say the grieving process lasts six months for every year you were together.

She was forty-two years old when he died and she never dated again. She begrudgingly went to one Parents Without Partners meeting and came home with some pamphlets and a coupon for three free karate lessons. She had eight hundred dollars in the bank, monthly social security checks, a job at a betting window at the racetrack. Everyone at the meeting seemed so plodding and glib, brimming with false light. Boys need positive male role models, a fellow partner-less parent told her at the meeting. She thought at first he was hitting on her, but it turned out he was recruiting boys for his martial arts dojo. Relieved, disappointed, she took the coupon he offered her. At River of Tradition we teach the four pillars of respect, he said, pointing to the patch on his coat, where the four pillars were listed. She wasn't wearing her glasses so she couldn't make them out, but it looked like one of them was CUSTARD. He's at an age where he should be working hard on his belief system, the man said, though she'd never told him how old I was.

My birthday parties, until I stopped having them, were always at Top Dogs. It had a special party room in the back and everyone got a foot-long except the birthday boy, who got a birthday footlong, which was just a footlong with special birthday toppings. I remember eating at Top Dogs a lot as a child, but I don't think we went there an unusual amount—I just remember every single trip there. The greasy, ass-buffed smoothness of the booth seats, the ritualized dressing of the footlong. Years after he died, when my mother was going through her born-again phase, she made us pray before we ate them. No one ever explained the mechanics of prayer to me, so I treated it like a wish list, closing my eyes and telling God everything I wanted. We quit one church for another and then quit church altogether, but the idea that I was born incomplete and that my natural inclinations are faulty, damnable even, has always rung true to me. Especially when I'm inside a Top Dogs. Our town council banned all fast-food chains within city limits, but the nearest Top Dogs isn't far. Just across the border in a grubby, makeshift red-light district: strip club, suspect massage parlor, marijuana factory outlet (ice cream man idling in the parking lot), Top Dogs. I eat quickly, hunched like a scavenger bird, and tell no one I've gone. I don't pray before eating my footlong but I tell myself that tomorrow I'll atone by running six miles instead of three. In my head I'm already running, absolving myself stride by stride for my casual trespasses into nostalgia.

In a booth nearby, a woman wearing a shredded golf visor says to another woman, Did you hear about the boy whose last wish was to die in Santa's lap? Turns out he was faking. It was just something he started saying and his parents went along with it. The other woman considers this and I sense everyone in our jetty of booths leaning in to hear her response. Top Dogs isn't the sort of place that abides deliberation—the woman's silence pulls at us like the branching limbo before a diagnosis. She reaches behind her ear and brings a tress of hair to her nose and sniffs at it. You know, she finally says, it's almost impossible to actually smell yourself.

Here's what I've been wondering, my mother said to me once over the phone. Here's what's been bugging me. Do you think he'd be dead by now if he didn't already die?

One year my sister and I dressed as boxes of laundry detergent for Halloween. She was Rinso, I was Biz. We made the costumes ourselves out of old cardboard boxes. Our mother thought it was so clever she sent a photo of us to the multinational conglomerate that manufactures Rinso and Biz and received, in return, a coupon for $1.50 off her next purchase. She was livid, she ranted about it for years afterward... but what had she expected? Free Rinso for life? She never could shed her unblinking faith in products she saw advertised on television. She knew Ivory was 99.44 percent pure and Calgon would take her away. When I was an infant she fed me Tang in a baby bottle because the commercials said it was healthy. The astronauts drank it, she'd say whenever she was pressed about feeding a newborn sugar water. That neon orange space powder rotted my baby teeth down to the root. Nowadays she watches the wholesale jewelry network, where the commercials are the show, and all the shows are about jewelry. She still wears her engagement ring, which she's had resized twice to fit her shrinking finger. The only other keepsake she has of my father, besides pictures, is his name on a yellowed slip of paper. After their first date she wrote it down and wedged it between her mattress and box spring because she heard that's what Janet Leigh did the night she met Tony Curtis.

Listening to my wife and son try to reach a compromise about how many toys he's allowed to bring to bed with him, I think: The sheer number of words it takes to raise a child—it's absurd. *Can*, I repeat when the song comes on. He *can* do anything. Escorting him through childhood on a flotilla of words. I remember the wannabe Amish guy who tended the video store cash register while his daughter lay next to him in a playpen. One night I came in and he was showing her trading cards with pictures of crying dwarves on them. Silently he'd hand her a card and silently she'd study it and hand it back to him. When he noticed me he said, I want to teach her that the world isn't as uncomplicated as she thinks it is.

A worthy enough goal, I guess. My son says he and a friend watched footage of ocean trenches, and there are these blind white eels that break apart if you bring them to the surface—they're held together by water pressure—and they terrified him. I tell him he shouldn't worry because he'll never have to go to the bottom of the ocean. You're better off worrying about the DMV, I say. He walks off without asking what *DMV* stands for, because he doesn't need to. His sense of danger is prehistoric, wiser than words.

* * *

And what to say about my half brother, my father's first son, who showed up at my college graduation and gave me a hundred-dollar bill in a bank envelope? He's ten years older than me, and I'd only met him a few times and haven't seen him since. He looked unnervingly like our father. He had a thin scar on his cheek and the skin on either side of it was misaligned, like patterned wallpaper not quite matched at the seam. The thing you should know about our dad (he told me when we were alone)—and you might not remember this because you were pretty young when he died—but that man was hung like a goddamn grandfather clock.

On my morning run, I often imagine myself at age eight watching me run past. There he goes again, I think of me thinking. When I was eight I found a switchblade in a crumpled paper bag. I also found, in the glove compartment of an abandoned mail truck in the woods, a porno magazine full of pregnant women. Something like that is bound to leave a permanent stain... and now that I'm thinking about it, what was a mail truck doing abandoned in the woods? I remember how on my school bus someone wrote *Black Sabbath Rules* on the back of the seat in front of mine, and every day I returned to check if they'd written anything else. I wanted a list. I wanted to know exactly what the Black Sabbath rules were.

I called a phone sex hotline I found in the magazine, made my voice good and deep. When the woman came on the line she said, *Well, well, well, well, Mr. Motherfucker.*

Our streets, they were here when we got here. They channel us, keep us from scribbling in the margins. Just before two city buses cross paths on Indian Hill, there's a moment when it's unclear whether or not the bus drivers will wave to each other. It lasts for about two seconds. When they do wave, the moment is neatly resolved, allowed to vaporize. When they don't, it lingers like a failed sneeze and expands into an omen, a placeholder for everything dreaded, all the things that could end badly and do. Next to my father in his Skylark, I used to signal to semitruck drivers on the highway, trying to get them to blow their air horns. I wanted influence, I wanted to be recognized by the biggest things on the road. I did this recently with my son in the car, and when the truck driver answered with a sustained honk, my son sank low in his seat, mortified. He made me promise to never do it again. I promised I would try. My son tells me I say *maybe* too much. He tells me that *we'll see* is not a satisfying answer. He's already eight years old, older than I was when I started to understand the subtle language of the road, the exonerating and implicating notes passed wordlessly from driver to driver to driver.

At IKEA he asks why there are so many pregnant women shopping and I tell him I'm not sure. He asks if women go to IKEA to get pregnant, and although I'm intrigued by the idea of women going to IKEA to get pregnant, I restrain myself from telling him that yes, they do. I say maybe they do. He asks if I knew that French women are naked 30 percent of the time, and I tell him I did not. Where did he hear this? He says it's just something he knows. He says he knows a lot of things his mother and I don't. It seems like lately he's been trying to keep himself a mystery. When I tell him he needs to go brush his teeth, he says, Does a tiger brush his teeth?

I know there are other things I should be showing him—truths, values, important concepts—but how can I if I'm still not clear on the particulars myself? The other day he asked what Captain Hook's name was before he lost his hand. I checked into Hook's details and read out his birth name to my son: James Aloysius Hook. His name was Hook before the hook—having his hand cut off and fed to a crocodile was a terrible irony. Or a coincidence. Or an ironic coincidence.

In college, I tell him, I had a friend named George Blaze. Guess how he died? My son covers his ears. He doesn't want to guess, or know, how George Blaze died. Later he asks me if there's such a thing as a monster planet. I ask him to clarify what he means and he says, A planet with only monsters on it. How am I supposed to answer a question like this? I answer yes. Which makes him happy (I knew it would) and a little apprehensive. How close is it? I pause for some quick calculations. At least ninety-seven light-years away, I tell him. Which is very far, I say. A light-year's like a normal year but much longer because it's a distance. You know how long a year feels, January to December? Okay, so imagine that but you're walking the entire time, through space. For ninety-seven years. That's how far.

He asks why it's called a light year and I say, No one's really sure, and put my hand on his shoulder, consoling him about all the things we want to know and cannot.

When my wife and I first met I told her I used to be pen pals with former president Ronald Reagan. She asked where the letters were and I tried to remember, growing annoyed at myself for being careless enough to misplace personal letters from former president Ronald Reagan, before remembering there were no letters. Truth is, I'd written to him once, after he tested the microphone at a radio address by saying, I've signed legislation to outlaw Russia forever. We begin bombing in five minutes. For a newly fatherless kid living fifty miles north of Cape Canaveral, which was a primary Russian target, who kept himself awake at night worrying about flash burn, air bursts, blast waves—phrases even the most unimaginative child could conjure viscerally—Reagan was a terrifying clown. The least he could have done was to write back and reassure me, tell me my fears were unreasonable. About a week later, I received a form letter on White House letterhead. I don't remember what it said. I read it quickly, licked my thumb and rubbed at the signature to see if it was real, then threw it away.

We are bears among the living, agile and fearsome. We range and rut. We hunt. We return to our dens to sleep and let torpid winters seal our wounds. When we die our pelts are stripped from our bones, draped over plausible likenesses, nailed to pedestals in telltale poses. Children still flinch at the sight of us, though our eyes are flat and lifeless. For now death seems to have perfectly arrested our essence. One day we're moved to the garage, replaced by a Christmas tree, and we stay there, surviving, yes, but shrinking. Time declaws us, softens our contours and our blood-matted fur, and it gives us a bow tie, and one day, where a life-size bear once stood, there's a cute little plush toy stuffed with foam and air, a harmless abbreviation consigned to spend a third life in the land of make-believe.

Sometimes I think I can I still summon the sound of his voice. A thin, distant rasp. My childhood is a song I've heard so many times I've stopped listening to the words. Probably half the things my father said to me he never said to me.

You're the man of the house now. Your duties consist of inward foraging, incubating petty grudges, and eating food before it expires. Fear not, I'll be watching over you until you're old enough to watch over yourself. Don't let that stop you from doing what, to the best of your knowledge, boys do. Become what you are, become what you are pretending to be. Learn something about everything and everything about something. Don't linger before mirrors. Appreciate rain. Take what scraps you have of me and raise them as a scarecrow against aspiring father figures. Make up some good shit. Never trust anyone who owns a reptile or a riding lawnmower. Is it my voice you're hearing right now or someone else's? And how old are you now? Old enough to watch over yourself? Old enough to watch over someone else? Children, and I quote, are the living messages we send to a time we will not see. Something along those lines. So what are you trying to say and why are you still trying to say it? Do you think this is a game, Kevin? Do you think you are winning?

THE MATING CALL

by MIKKEL ROSENGAARD

ON THE INTERNET, AS you probably know, there was a copy of a
South Seas island where everything was rendered in natural size, and
so lifelike that it looked like the genuine thing.

The real island is one of the prettiest in the world. A landscape
of swaying palm trees, white-sand beaches, teeming coral reefs under
an azure sea, and so far away, and so difficult to reach, that only the
very rich can get there. That is precisely why the art collector commissioned the copy. He wanted everyone to see it, even the poor who
never have a chance to travel.

On the art collector's island, you could see all the wonders of the
South Seas. Waves always lapped gently against the beach. The sky
was ever-blue. Yes, the island was so artfully rendered, and stretched
so far, that not even the animator had been to all its corners. In the
jungle you could see the strangest orchids. Monkeys howled from the
canopy. And if you kept on walking, a path led up through the hills
to a caldera lake that was deep and blue. Old trees were mirrored in
the water, and among the branches lived an ʻōʻō bird who sang so

wistful a mating call that even a young gamer, playing a tournament late at night, stopped his game and listened when he heard the ʻōʻō calling from the open tab. "Holy shit. What a beautiful song," he said.

Visitors came from all around the internet to admire the island's beaches and jungles and the caldera lake. And if they happened to hear the mating call, they breathed: "Beautiful!"

The visitors told their followers about the extraordinary island. They posted screenshots of the beaches and the jungles, but nothing was shared more often than the ʻōʻō's mating call. Those who knew how to edit videos uploaded gorgeous shots of the island, all featuring the ʻōʻō's song.

Those videos spread across the world, and some of them eventually reached the art collector. He sat in his art foundation's study, scrolling and scrolling as he nodded approvingly, because he believed in truth and nature and nothing pleased him more than to share the true beauty of the South Seas.

"Wow, that mating call," said the top comment. "That's the prettiest thing I ever heard."

"What is this all about?" said the art collector. "A mating call. And supposedly the best thing on my entire island?"

And then he opened a window to the island and walked from the beach up the hills to the caldera lake. When he reached the shore, he noticed a melancholy little warble. Sure enough, it was the ʻōʻō singing its mating call so longingly that the art collector drew a deep breath. Tears crept into his eyes, and then the ʻōʻō's song sounded even sadder and more wistful. The art collector sighed and thought about all the poor people who lived among such ugly things and would never have heard so beautiful a song if it hadn't been for his generosity.

"I've never heard anything so beautiful," said the art collector. "And to think this is just a copy! The whole internet loves the online bird, but I would like to hear the genuine thing."

The art collector chartered a flight and flew the long way to the island in the South Seas. And because he was such a generous man, he invited his colleagues and family to come along. The first day they saw the beaches and the coral reefs.

"Ah," said the museum director. "I know this place! It feels exactly like I've been here before."

The second day they saw the jungle.

"Gorgeous!" said the critic. "I'm seeing it for the first time, but it's like a déjà vu."

The third day they visited the caldera lake.

"Down here!" cried the art collector's granddaughter when they reached the ridge. "Look! Look! Now we'll hear the birdie." And off she ran down the path toward the shore where ancient trees were mirrored in the lake.

"No luck today, I guess," said the museum director, when they had circled the lake without hearing the mating call.

"Dear little 'ō'ō," whispered the granddaughter, "come along, come along. We wish only to hear your pretty song."

But there was no mating call to be heard, only the wind whistling in the trees.

That evening the art collector held a dinner, and the dining hall was decorated with torches and the loveliest flowers. The museum director gave a speech and declared the online island a groundbreaking work of internet art. The critic lauded the island for how closely the real jungle resembled the forests online. Oh yes, the island was certainly a success! The art collector beamed with pride.

"I don't think I've ever been as happy as on this gorgeous island," he said.

All that was missing was the 'ō'ō's song. But when the art collector asked the hotel staff what time of day they could hear the mating call, they had no clue what he was talking about. They had lived in town all their life. They knew only the ashen birds that lived among the houses, and were not familiar with the jungle birds.

"How sad," said the art collector. "All this nature in their back-yard and they don't even know the 'ō'ō's mating call. That's the problem with kids today. They always have their eyes glued to a screen."

He sent his personal assistant to get advice on how they could hear the 'ō'ō's song. But where was the mating call to be found? The PA ran up and down streets, in and out of travel agencies. Not a single person she met knew where they could hear the 'ō'ō's song. The PA ran back to the art collector and said that the mating call must be a feature fabricated by the animator. "That's how it goes with game designers. You should not believe everything they animate. It's all invention and what's called Easter eggs."

"Easter eggs?" said the art collector. "No, my island is an exact copy of the real island. If there is no 'ō'ō in real life, there should not be one online."

And then the art collector called the animator, who was so busy with his rigging and modeling that he did not hear the phone ring.

"But the animator has won prizes and grants for his accurate depictions," the art collector said. "So it has to be real. No, I want to hear that mating call. And it better be soon, because in three days we are flying home."

"Of course," said the PA, and once again she searched the island for the strange bird that the whole internet knew about but no one had laid eyes on. She walked up and down the island streets. She drove down potholed roads and clambered up muddy paths.

Finally, deep in the jungle, the PA met a poor old woman. The woman said: "Ah yes, the 'ō'ō? Of course, I know him very well."

The old woman told the story of the 'ō'ō. When the white people arrived, they brought mosquitoes to the island. With the mosquitoes, diseases arrived. Every year, birds died. And in the end only a single 'ō'ō was left.

"He lived up by the lake in a tree hollow before he died," said the old lady. "And when I walked home in the evening I would hear him calling for his mate. I had to sit and whistle a reply. Because the song of the 'ō'ō is a duet, and no mate would ever answer his call."

Back at the hotel, the art collector nodded slowly as he listened to the story. Tears gathered in his eyes, for he knew what it was like to call out for the one you love and never receive a reply. "Was anyone ever as lonesome as that poor 'ō'ō?" asked the art collector over dinner, and the museum director and the critic shook their heads as sadly as they could.

The next morning the art collector woke up with a new idea.

"I will resurrect the mating call," he said, because he had always believed in conserving nature, and in love as well.

Back in his study at the art foundation, he posted an open call and promised that any artist who could figure out how to re-create the mating call on the island in the South Seas would receive a prize.

In studios across the world, sculptors and animators and video artists considered how to solve the problem. Solar-powered speakers? Robotic birds? The whole art world gossiped about the strange assignment. Even the critical theorists and radical de-colonialists were excited, and that is saying a lot, because they were rarely pleased.

One day, after many months, a courier delivered a package to the art collector. The label said MATING CALL.

"So, another robo-bird," said the art collector when he saw the birdcage inside the package. But it was not a robot. A real living being sat on the perch, a little bird with yellow feathers and a beating heart. The instructions told him to whistle to the bird, and as soon as he did, the bird began to warble. The art collector closed his eyes, and its song filled the room. The notes rose and fell, as wistful as the song he had heard so often by the online lake. Yes, it really was the mating call! A golden plate was attached to the birdcage. On it were the words THE YELLOW-CRESTED FLYCATCHER STREAMS THE LONGING OF THE 'ō'ō.

"How is it possible? It's a different bird, but it knows the melody?" said the art collector.

The young artist who had sent the package was at once summoned to the art foundation. She explained that she had been born in the South Seas herself, but on a different island, where the yellow-crested flycatcher lived. The flycatcher did not sound very much like the ʻōʻō. Its song was happier, not nearly as wistful as the mating call from the online island. But the flycatcher was a skilled imitator and a quick learner too. Perhaps, she'd thought, if she played the mating call to a hatchling, it could learn to imitate the ʻōʻō's call.

So the artist had acquired a baby flycatcher. She placed a tablet in the birdcage, and every morning and every night, and every afternoon as well, she kept a window open to the online island. She covered the birdcage with a blanket so the flycatcher could see nothing but the ancient trees and hear nothing but the mating call by the caldera lake. The flycatcher grew big and strong by the warm glow of the tablet screen. And one morning the artist heard it singing a mating call just like the one online.

"It's beautiful," whispered the art collector, and the critic and the museum director agreed. A real living bird that sang an extinct love song—what a poetic gesture! "Otherworldly! Mellifluous! Chthonic!" they said, and the young artist who had taught the flycatcher to sing was immediately awarded a fellowship as resident artist of the art foundation.

"You have resurrected the mating call," said the museum director to the art collector. "Now the island in the South Seas will once again sound like it did in the old, unspoiled days."

Soon the flycatcher was released on the island, and all day the yellow bird sat alone in the ancient trees and sang his lonely song. His mating call sounded wistful and melancholy, but not exactly like the song online.

"Well, that's the beauty of natural things," said the critic. "They all have their quirks and peculiarities and what we call charms."

On the real island, tourists heard about the songbird with the wistful mating call. They hiked out to the caldera lake to listen.

Travel agencies arranged birding tours. Soon the flycatcher's song brought as much joy to people as the mating call online, and on top of that the real bird was so much more fun to photograph. It flew about and caught flies and puffed up its yellow breast.

The critic wrote a monograph about the living bird. It was so complicated, and so full of references to the most difficult theories, that all the other critics published rave reviews, because otherwise they might have seemed crude and been mocked online. The critic assured the art collector that the flycatcher was even better than the 'ō'ō, not just in terms of its mating call, but also because it was so much more authentic, with its genuine feathers and real living eyes.

"We always know exactly what comes out of the internet bird," said the critic. "Everything is decided by an algorithm—it sounds like *this*, and never any other way. But with the real living bird, you cannot calculate its song. It has character, and if you were to slit it open, there would be no strings of code determining how it sings. Because it is guided by a bigger force, by what we call life."

Oh yes, the flycatcher was certainly a marvel! The art collector commissioned a documentary about the real living bird by the caldera lake. "The poor people should also have a chance to hear the genuine thing," said the art collector. And when people streamed the documentary they were so pleased that they left hundreds of comments. They wrote, "Aww!" and posted hearts and tiny smiling faces. But the young gamer who had so often heard the online mating call said: "It looks cute, and it does sound totally like it, but something is off. I wonder what it is?"

A whole year went by. All across the island, tour guides and hotel staff told the story of the extraordinary bird that had brought an extinct love song back to life. There were souvenirs and postcards featuring the flycatcher. And every week, more and more tourists came to the island from far away to hear the famous mating call. A rapper composed lyrics about the lonely 'ō'ō who would never find his love. The whole island hummed the song. If two heartbroken lovers met, all one of them had to say was "Oh, oh," and they would sigh and feel each other's longing. Travel bloggers took photos and retold the story of the lonesome bird, and one of these stories reached an ornithologist many thousands of miles away, who was lying on his couch scrolling his phone.

"What kind of mess is this," he mumbled, and jumped up from the couch to pull down volumes from his library. He was an endowed professor, and so wise that he never opened his mouth without getting paid for it, but this story made him so upset that he went straight to work without even a contract or expense account. And after much leafing through zoological nomenclatures, and much referencing of taxonomies, he wrote a letter to the art collector to explain that no 'ō'ō had ever lived on the green island in the blue South Seas. "I have visited this island many times, I have studied its fauna, I know all of its birds," the professor wrote. "And I can guarantee you that the 'ō'ō and its mating call are fake."

"But I heard about it myself," said the art collector when he called the ornithologist. "I heard it from the island's oldest woman. And she was a proper native too! So what do you mean the mating call is fake?"

"————!" said the professor and hung up, because his expertise no longer came for free.

The call had disturbed the art collector. How could the endowed professor accuse him of being fake? He, who cared so much about the truth, and who had spent a fortune to share genuine natural beauty with the poor? Once again, he called the animator, who suffered from toothaches and had traveled south to get a dental bridge, for he did not have health insurance and could not afford the dentists in his homeland. The art collector left an angry message asking where the animator had gotten the 'ō'ō from. He sent text messages and a cease and desist order, but the animator received none of it, for he did not have phone coverage abroad.

The art collector summoned the endowed professor. The scholar got his contract and expense account, and got to work. He called the top ornithologists. Anthropologists and ethnographers also got involved, even a professor in cognitive psychology. All of them interviewed the poor old woman in the jungle.

The anthropologist concluded that the poor old woman spoke in allegories. The psychology professor diagnosed her with advanced dementia. In any case, the experts agreed that the old woman was not talking about a real living bird, but about an ancient myth: the one about the bird who sings his final mating call before this world ends and a new world arises.

"Find that animator," cried the art collector. "And I mean right now, because I am pissed off!"

"Of course," said the PA, who continued calling the dental offices of the southern neighbor. Finally, she found the animator, and after much pleading and many threats of litigation, he admitted that the mating call was not a natural song. Late one night on the internet, the animator had seen a video about the mythical ʻōʻō. He'd thought the legend so beautiful that he had asked his niece—who was a DJ on the weekends—if she would sample him a mating call.

"Oh, god," said the art collector when he heard the story. "I have spread a false song. An artificial mating call that never belonged in nature."

The art collector called the governor of the island and explained that the mating call was a fabrication.

"If you help me catch the flycatcher," said the art collector, "I promise I will delete the online island and the fake mating call, and never again will I interfere with your community."

"Don't be silly," said the governor. "Your island has done us a lot of good. You keep your online island, and we will keep the mating call. But please promise me one thing—please don't tell anyone it was made by a teenage girl."

"Politicians," mumbled the art collector. "They have no sense of the true and the genuine. They only care about the next election."

And then he called the hotelier who had hosted him during his stay.

"Please," said the art collector. "Please help me stop this false mating call."

The hotelier turned on his phone's video and showed the art collector his hotel. The swimming pool was packed. Every chair in his restaurant was taken up by hungry diners. And why were they so hungry? Because they had spent the whole day hiking, searching for the mating call.

"Look at them!" said the hotelier. "For them the mating call is real enough."

"Businessmen," muttered the art collector. "They have no sense of the authentic and the real. The only thing they care about is money." And then he called for his PA to summon the endowed professor.

"Professor, please. Do something before the whole island gets infected with this artificial song."

"————," said the professor, and so the art collector had to go and get his checkbook.

The endowed professor got straight to work. And after many phone calls and much referencing of legal codes, he concluded that it was illegal to hunt wild birds on the island. "But no need to fear," he said. "Within a decade, I promise you, all chirping on the island will be real and natural again."

All they had to do was wait and the mating call would die out on its own. After all, there was only a single yellow-crested flycatcher, and he could not mate alone.

Ten years! And all that time the artificial song would stain and soil the pristine jungles of the virgin island. What a horrible shame! "You poor, unspoiled island," said the art collector and bowed his head in embarrassment. "Look at you, drowning in tourists and inauthentic song, and all of it is my fault."

Ten years passed, and the whole art world was worried because everyone was fond of the generous art collector. Now rumors said he had fallen ill. His formidable art collection had been donated to museums. The board of his company had already appointed a new CEO. Only doctors and psychiatrists were allowed to visit his sickbed, and even the strongest drugs could no longer lighten his mood.

All day long the art collector lay in his bed, pale and rigid, while the doctors discussed his treatment. The chief psychiatrist advised him to take a convalescent holiday by the sea, far from the city's noise and screens. "Where have you been the calmest and the happiest?" she asked, but the art collector was so weak and dazed that he could not reply.

"I know," said the PA. "I know where he was the happiest."

The whole long way to the South Seas, the art collector dozed. He was so drowsy from the drugs that he did not even notice when they laid him in a bed in a magnificent tree house high in the jungle canopy. In the treetop hotel, the hotelier had left the windows open all around, so the art collector could sleep in the freshest air. The Wi-Fi had been switched off, the power cut, and that's why it was so quiet that only the sounds of the jungle could be heard—so quiet that the PA had to put her hand in front of the art collector's lips to check if he was breathing.

But the art collector was still alive. Dazed and confused, he woke up late at night in the dim treetop bedroom high above the jungle. Next to the bed, a panoramic window was open, and below him the palm trees swayed in the night.

"Where am I?" whispered the art collector. "Why is it so dark?"

Just then the clouds broke and the moon shone on the island. The art collector stumbled out of bed, and when he saw the beach and the jungle and the caldera lake, he could hardly breathe. From the dark trees he heard a synthetic sound.

"'Ō'ō!" called a voice.

"'Ō'ō!" called another voice and then another, "'Ō'ō!" From all around the forest he heard the digital call, and sweat poured down his neck.

"Turn it off," said the art collector. "Turn off that fakeness!"

But through the window, the beach and the forest and the crater lake were still bathed in the pale moonlight, there was no button to switch off, and the panorama window had no screen.

"Turn it off, turn it off," screamed the art collector, and he threw a fist into the window, and as his arm went through the frame, he lost his balance. He tripped through the open window, and fell screaming through the canopy. The PA heard his shriek. The hotelier heard bones and branches snap and crack.

"An accident!" cried the PA.

"A suicide!" said the hotelier.

But the poor art collector was not dead. He lay on the forest floor with fractured arms and legs and stared up into the entangled vines. On a little heap of twigs sat two birds rubbing beaks. One was yellow-crested. The other was ashen, its little chest throbbing in an electronic rhythm.

The hotelier and the PA came running to find the art collector's body. There he lay among the old trees, and as they approached, he raised a shaking hand and pointed at the nest.

"'Ō'ō!" called the yellow bird.

"'Ō'ō!" answered the ashen one and sat down on her eggs.

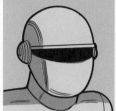

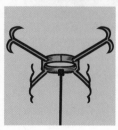

DREAM OF AN AFRO PESSIMIST

BY MICHAEL KENNEDY

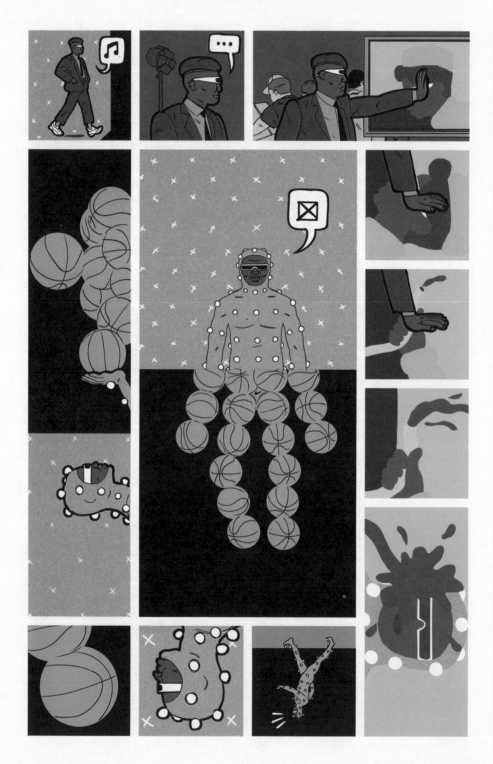

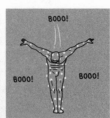

FIELD NOTES

by Adam Iscoe

IT RAINED THE NEXT day and the day after that it also rained. I stopped biking at a gas station about fifteen miles from Progreso, Texas, to get out of the storm. Two carnitas tacos and a carne asada bought me two hours in a green plastic folding chair inside, next to the auto repair aisle. Motor oil, jumper cables, Snickers bars. Across the store, hot dogs turned around and around. There was an outlet to charge my phone.

I was too tired to catch up on email or read the news, so I sat there watching people buy gas and energy drinks as morning turned to afternoon. Eventually, it stopped raining and I asked the woman who made the tacos if I could bathe in the restroom sink. "If it suits you," she said. I washed my face, body, and socks twice. Then my socks again. When I went outside afterward, I noticed that a man I had seen in the gas station bathroom an hour earlier was sitting in his car out front. A big man, both tall and fat, long white socks and long black hair, the side of his head shaved bald.

When he opened his car door to speak with me, I saw he was wearing black gym sandals with the Texas flag printed on them. He wasn't smoking, but his car smelled like he had been. I asked him for directions to the fire station. He told me, then asked how come. I told him that's where I hoped to pitch my tent for the night. He said he was on his way to pick up his dead sister's kids from elementary school. I didn't know why he told me his sister was dead.

"I'm still paying for her funeral," he said. "It was hard because our family wanted to see her in an open casket. She told me, 'Hey, just cremate me, I know you don't have that much money,' and I said, 'Okay,' but they wanted to see her, so I made it like that." He told me it must have cost almost three thousand dollars for everything, the flowers, the open casket, just to do it right. "So now I'm paying it. I think I still owe fourteen hundred dollars," he said. "But the guy who lent us the money was pretty cool, and we know him, so it was all right."

A motorcycle pulled up next to us, and I strained to hear him over the sound of the engine. He told me he was now a father to seven children—three of his own, plus four from his sister. "I tell 'em, 'I'm still your uncle, but you can call me Dad if you want.'" They all lived in a three-bedroom, seventy-three-foot-long single-axle trailer, not too far from here, he said, and he was going to quit his job soon because his wife's job paid better and she needed the car to get to work while he was at home taking care of the little ones. I wondered what it was like for him to pick those children up at school. I wondered what it felt like to drive them home instead of over to his sister's place. But I didn't ask him about any of that. Instead, I just listened as he said, "I love them—that's what keeps me going." And then he showed me a picture of the children on his phone, we introduced ourselves, and he said he'd better head out. "Maybe, I don't know, maybe I'll see you somewhere else," he said.

* * *

I told the grant committee my project would update John Steinbeck's novel *Travels with Charley: In Search of America*, only instead of driving around the country in a GMC pickup truck with two rifles, a compact encyclopedia, and a French poodle named Charley in the passenger seat, I would ride my bicycle. And I would do it alone. I had not yet read the novel when I sat at the head of a long oak table to make my case. Truth be told, the grant proposal was mostly a distraction from the mundanity of my life at the time. I didn't expect to receive the money. I just wanted to win something.

I wore a blue tie; there was a glass of water on the table and seven committee members seated around it. Steinbeck's novel is famous, so I figured the committee would be eager to fund the idea. You know, a year spent traveling around the country on a bicycle with a tape recorder interviewing "ordinary" people in order to better understand the "texture" of the nation's cities, towns, and faraway places. What is America? What does it mean to call ourselves Americans? Someone at the far end of the table rolled their eyes when I said I planned to spend the grant money (and the next year or two of my life) "searching" for America. Then someone else laughed. Oh well, I thought as I walked home.

A few months later, I was killing time before work outside a Chick-fil-A when I received an email announcing I had won the grant. More than enough money to spend a year on the road. Cash money; holy shit. I bought an extra-large chocolate milkshake and waffle fries to celebrate.

Snowstorm, thunderstorm, heat wave, headwind. For more than a year, each day brought gravel paths and busy four-lane highways, farm-to-market roads, and muddy detours. Late afternoon meant I asked for directions on the side of the road. And then I pitched my tent behind the police station or a little church; next to cemeteries, water towers, cell phone towers, radio towers; alongside the highway, in the woods. Sometimes I laid out my bedroll inside a fire station or community center or high school gym.

A few months into my travels, I found myself riding along a two-lane South Carolina road called Heritage Highway, redbud and dogwood and sweet bay growing thick on either side. The road, like most in the area, looped and bent around itself; creeks, rivers, kudzu, oaks. My legs ached, my back ached, my hands were numb. I'd long since given up on searching for America. The sky had turned the color of soured milk, and the forecast called for heavy rain again that night.

There weren't many people around; it was easy to get lost, but at least I had cell service. I pulled over and telephoned the fire department in a town twenty-something miles up the road to see if they had anywhere dry for me to stay the night. It had worked the night before, in Blackville, and I figured it might work here, near Saint George, another medium-size town with lots of churches along US Highway 78. I told the woman on the other end of the phone that my tent had sprung a leak and the thunderstorm had already started up and did she think I could spend the night at the station? Maybe the post office? The folks in Blackville had let me stay at their community center, I said. The woman sounded sympathetic when she said, "No, sorry, we can't allow that, honey. Best of luck to you."

I sat there under a willow for a few minutes to get out of the rain, trying my best to ignore the lonely voice at the back of my head.

I got a call a few hours later and the same voice said, "Ms. Mary Murray would like to put you up at the Econo Lodge." The world simplified; I didn't mind the weather anymore. I rode cheerfully through Bamberg and Reevesville, past a paper mill and a Chinese food restaurant, over the Edisto River and Cattle Creek, and into Saint George.

I was soaking wet when a white-haired woman in a floral shirt and pressed blue jeans arrived at the motel in a white Chevy Impala. "It's a pleasure to meet you," I said. I thanked her for coming down here, and explained I was not homeless so much as traveling for months on my bicycle, and that maybe the money should be spent elsewhere because I still had some left. To which Ms. Mary Murray said: "You shouldn't turn down a gift from God."

I had left my childhood home in Texas with little more than the ambition to write a grand American travelogue. I had only the vague outline of a plan: use the grant money to buy food and the occasional night in a motel; ride as many miles per day as possible for as long as possible; and record my conversations on a tape recorder. Months later, even after I had abandoned my half-baked project, I tried to ask the people I met (at the grocery store, on the side of the road, atop a river bluff, or aboard a ferry boat) to tell me a story, because, usually, before too long, they would then offer me a dry place to sleep. Behind the barn, in the barn, in the backyard, in the basement, "Why don't you go ahead and take the guest bedroom downstairs?" I wonder what they noticed about me while I noticed them. My hair, my clothes, the way I walked in my shoes, the sound of my stomach? I have always been able to recognize the lonesome, and, I think, the lonesome have always been able to recognize me.

It wasn't a surprise when I walked up to a church in Bussey, Iowa, and the pastor invited me to spend the night inside. He introduced himself as Andy Tuttle. He had bright eyes and a white, square beard. I asked him, How're you doing, and he said just fine. "I'm doing fine," he said, which is what I've noticed most people say when things are not fine. And so I asked him, How are you really doing, no, I mean it, how're you really doing? He didn't answer at first. He just told me I could sleep on the pews, but when he told this to his wife, Deborah, she insisted he invite me for dinner in their home. I was sitting on their couch in front of an old flat-screen TV eating a Walmart pizza and fish sticks when I remembered you were dead.

There were three cars and a truck rusting next to a basketball hoop in the pastor's yard, and a deer carcass hanging from a hook in the garage. "That's what we'll eat all winter," he said as I went to put my bike away. "Deborah has fibromyalgia. I'm the only source of income for us, and as a pastor you might guess I don't make much. We don't make much but I'm a good hunter and Thad here is homeschooled, so he's learning to hunt too." He motioned to the doorway; his son was standing just outside. The three of us joined Deborah inside to watch a football game in the living room. She and I shared the couch; Thad sat on the floor. I can't remember who was playing whom. The volume on the TV was turned down, and the announcer's voice emerged from a weather radio next to the couch.

Andy Tuttle told me he used to be a drug addict, as someone made a field goal on the flat screen. "It was a rough-and-tumble time," he said. "I was pretty much into playing music and drinking too much. I was taking a lot of speed, too, so I could drink more than a person should—a whole case of beer and most of a fifth. Most nights, we'd be out until three or four and then I'd get up at six and do the whole thing again." He said he got sick. Not from drinking, but sick-sick, he said. "That's when things changed for me." He told me he found God, and God made him well. He was flat on his back, he said, when the Lord brought him back to life. I thought about you lying in the middle of a busy avenue in 2011. Collapsed lung, fractured skull; brain-dead. An ambulance picked you up and took you to the hospital. A few days later, your parents pulled the plug and I gave up on God.

By the time the pastor finished his first story, I had stopped listening. Sadness had welled up in me. You were on your back in the middle of an eight-lane avenue, and then you were gone, and I didn't have it in me to listen anymore. I wanted to sob in a bathtub, my bathtub, but I didn't have a bathtub anymore, only a bicycle, so I just sat there trying to be a good houseguest as one of the teams scored another touchdown. Thad cheered. I nodded for the rest of the night, pretending to listen to Andy's stories like a polite child visiting his great-aunt. Deborah sensed something was wrong and apologized, thinking it had to do with her house. "I just wish things were perfect," she said. But despite the sadness haunting me, it was perfect. All the old papers and trash piled in odd places reminded me of Dad's house in Texas. I told her it was perfect, it's perfect, it's perfect here. Deborah smiled with her bottom teeth. As I said good-night, she warned, "The shower drains real slow!" I slept well for the first time in a long time. When I woke in the middle of the night to pee, Andy was still awake, studying the Bible in a cracked green leather recliner in his living room. He watched me watching him from the hall. A few hours later, we ate frozen waffles for breakfast. Deborah asked if I had any questions for them about God. I did not ask why he took you from us.

When your house caught on fire, one fall in middle school, the insurance company put your whole family up in a room at the Embassy Suites. It was your birthday. Your folks let us order a chocolate cake from room service and we jumped around singing songs until your dad told us to go to sleep. A few months later, we learned to shoot rifles and play cards in a green four-walled canvas tent a few miles from town, at Boy Scout camp. I remember there was a big thunderstorm, and we took turns peeing out the door of the tent so we wouldn't have to walk through the mud to the woods. Then we grew up and apart. You quit Boy Scouts; I went to a different high school. Up and apart, and then you ran away from home. I remember your mom called my mom in a weeklong effort to track you down. And when you did come home, your parents sent you to one of those wilderness camps for "troubled" teenagers. You were in Henderson, Nevada, when you ran away again. I guess you left the first chance you got.

A few weeks before I met Ms. Mary Murray at the Econo Lodge, while I was riding through eastern Mississippi, a blond woman with a mole on her neck flagged me down in front of her gas station restaurant and said a man named Ronald Byrd had seen me riding this morning and had called ahead to make sure my next meal was on him. "Anything you want," she said. I ordered the lunch special: pork chop, potatoes, grits, coleslaw, cornbread, and a slice of chocolate cake. As I was cleaning my plate, the woman, Ms. Kay, said, "You be careful, now, a cyclist got hit by a truck or something not too far from here—it killed him."

A lady sitting at a table near mine said, "Yeah, I remember that."

"He was a real sweet kid. I never met him. I read about it, what a sad deal. He was raising money for cancer, I think, isn't that right?"

"Yeah, I think that was it," the second lady said. "You be careful, you hear me?"

I said, Yes, ma'am to both of them.

"I'm serious," Ms. Kay said. "You be safe, now, on these roads, these log trucks don't slow down for nobody and even us regular drivers can't see over these hills—it's just dangerous roads. Please be careful, baby—"

I said I was nothing except careful out there.

Just the night before, I'd had almost the exact same conversation. A late-1960s Pontiac pulled over on the side of Mississippi Highway 42 at the top of a big hill. I was still at the bottom of the hill when the car stopped. It took me a while to reach it and when I did the driver-side window was rolled down. There was a wooden cane in the passenger seat and a folded-up walker in the back. I was in a lousy mood when the driver asked, "Where are ya headed?"

I told him.

"You've gotta be careful, son. Log trucks on this road wouldn't think twice about running you over dead. We lost a cyclist a few years ago, down on Highway 98, and I don't know what happened but—"

I interrupted him and said, Don't you tell me that.

"Well, it's true."

I said, I don't want to know about any of that if I'm gonna be riding these roads out here.

"Just want you to be careful, is all, it's not safe out here on this road with these trucks—"

I lied and told him I was managing just fine.

"Where you sleeping tonight?"

I said I didn't quite know, maybe the woods past Rich—what's the town I'm thinking of called? It's so hot out here I can hardly even—

"Richton?"

Yeah, Richton.

"Well, I'll tell you what—if you decide you want it, and I'm not saying you've gotta, but if you decide you want you can come over to my place and camp or whatever you'd like there, just past a big tower like this one, but bigger—"

He pointed to a cell phone tower among the pine trees.

"—just past the big tower there'll be a church and past that a road, make a left there, it's not quite four miles from Richton and we're the fourth house down there on the left. Got it?"

I wasn't listening; I was too tired to listen anymore. I asked if he had an address I could put into Google Maps.

"It doesn't show up on Maps. Well, not on the car Maps. Maybe your phone will have it better, yeah, put in 'Union Road' and see if it comes up."

I did not have any service.

"Does it come up there?"

I said it did, though it did not.

"Okay, well, the road's called Union Road. Just look out for it and just look out for my car in the front, you shouldn't have any trouble."

He drove on down the road. I sat in the shade cast by a volunteer fire station near where he had stopped, and caught my breath for fifteen minutes. Maybe it was an hour. What I remember most is the heat. When I got going again, it wasn't five minutes before a little red Hyundai full of older guys passed me and shouted, "Fuck you, man, get off the road!" Afterward, two log trucks came barreling along, one right after the other, pine trees dangling out the back, almost low enough to scrape the ground, and I almost went off into the ditch from the wind they cast. If I had stuck my left hand halfway out, it would have been ripped clean off. I kept riding two, three, four miles at least until I saw the cell phone tower and turned left at Union Road. David Hamontree was seated on a lawn tractor, mowing his front yard in his pajamas. Blue-and-black-striped flannel pajamas in the one-hundred-degree heat. He waved for me to come around down the long dirt driveway, and shouted over the engine, "I'm gonna go put this mower in the shed, why don't you just wait here for a second." I sat on a wooden swing he said he'd built by hand, and waited to be invited inside.

David's wife, Tillie, came out with a Styrofoam cup full of iced tea, and for dinner we enjoyed homemade spaghetti sauce with garlic bread she had made earlier that week. The bread was still half-frozen when she put it on my plate. David had changed into red flannel pajama bottoms and a blue T-shirt. As we ate, the couple took turns telling me I should stay for another day or two—"even a week," Tillie said, offering me the guest room. "If you wait a week, David can drive you all the way to Georgia." David said he could get me as far as South Carolina. He was going to be delivering an early batch of peaches, he said, and he wouldn't mind the conversation, or the detour, so long as it wasn't more than a couple hundred miles out of his way. In the morning, after breakfast, I think I surprised them when I said goodbye. I didn't tell them about the lonely voice in my head.

It had been chasing me for months, from post offices to county parks to cash-only motels, mile after mile like the whistle of a freight train in the wind. Sometimes I could hardly hear it; other times it was impossible to ignore. I should've stayed a day or a week and helped David lift the peaches and then his electric wheelchair into the back of his truck and driven with him through Mississippi, Alabama, Georgia, South Carolina, and back to his house again. I should've asked him about picking cotton as a kid, when he lived along the Mississippi River, and I should've asked Tillie what she thought about the legacy of slavery in the South. She had told me her great-great-grandparents owned slaves and I wondered but did not have it in me to ask what she thought about that. I should've asked her, What are you most proud of in this life? and, Of what are you most ashamed? Should've, though I did not. It felt more natural to ride my bicycle through the heat and wonder, Did you hear the same lonely voice, in the days before the car hit you? Or is it mine alone?

You know, I've always thought it wasn't an accident. That you wanted that speeding car to strike you dead. Your parents pulled the plug at the hospital because the accident had left you brain-dead, but in my mind, at least, you took your own life. You stepped into oncoming traffic on South Eastern Avenue, north of St. Rose Parkway, at 12:30 p.m. on Saturday, July 9, 2011, in Henderson, Nevada.

After crossing the Chickasawhay River, I got a flat tire near State Line, Mississippi. My third in four days. I sat beneath a magnolia, cursing under my breath. It wasn't long before a white Toyota Corolla pulled over and woman with hair the color of brown sugar got out. She asked what I was doing, and, once I explained, offered to help fix my tire. Though I had fixed flat bicycle tires hundreds of times, I accepted. I was exhausted. Anyone who says the southeastern US is flat terrain is telling you a lie; the hills felt like mountains in the heat. It took only a few minutes because she had a portable air compressor in the back seat. Once we'd fixed the tire, the woman drove away and I rode to a convenience store in town. There were a few people sitting on wooden pallets out front.

I went inside to buy some beef jerky and a Gatorade. A man in a tank top bought beer, and the woman behind me in line, skinny, with tattoos on her forearms, handed me a few dollars and some spare change. "Buy yourself a cold drink, baby," she said. "My stepdad was in the military—I understand how hard all this traveling is." I had received countless small kindnesses while traveling, but no one had ever just handed me cash. Dumbstruck, I followed her outside with my Gatorade and we chatted for a while behind her Mustang about nothing in particular until a lady in shorts told us to get moving 'cause we were hogging the pump. I wrote down her name, Agnes Debra Williams, so I wouldn't ever forget.

I rested there on the pallets for a while, watching the gas station like one might watch birds or an approaching storm. An overweight drunk woman asked me if I had half a dollar; a middle-aged man with pronounced veins and a big buck knife hanging from a bejeweled belt won a few dollars playing a scratcher; a logger with teeth like a spiral staircase said the only thing harder than logging was the heat. I agreed, Yes, sir, then asked him for directions, and when I started heading the wrong way a few minutes later, he shouted down the road to get me back on course. No more than ten minutes later, a man named Kurt Johnson, who was pulling a Kawasaki Mule in a trailer behind a new Ford pickup, stuck twenty dollars out his window and said, "Jesus love you, I love you, next meal on me."

A few hours later, I sat down for dinner with Cindy and Carl Craig at their home in Chatom, Alabama. Chicken, hamburgers, corn on the cob, potatoes, a salad, cornbread, *and* dinner rolls. Another feast. Their home was air-conditioned. I drank a beer; we made small talk. The house smelled familiar, like the soap your mom used when we were growing up. I drank a second beer, and a third, and told them about all the good turns I had received the last few days. David and Tillie's house; the restaurant meal; cash pressed into my hand twice in ten minutes before the Alabama state line; this, right here, sitting in the living room with y'all. I wondered aloud if any of it had to do with this other cyclist I had heard about, whom everyone seemed to have known or at least had heard of—you know, the one who died. Carl avoided my eyes. Cindy said they'd met the young man, James Dobson, the same way she'd met me—on a website called WarmShowers.org, a kind of Facebook built to connect long-distance bicyclists with a couch, a spare room, or a hot meal. James had also enjoyed hamburgers at her kitchen table and a night's rest in their comfortable guest bedroom. Overstuffed pillows, handmade quilt. A driver in a 2016 Dodge Challenger had hit James as they both headed west on US Highway 98 near Hattiesburg, Mississippi, on a Tuesday afternoon, only a few hours after he left Cindy and Carl's house. Volunteer firefighters arrived within minutes. He was pronounced dead at the scene.

Cindy told me she remembered getting a text message. "That's how I found out," she said. "Someone wrote, 'Was that cyclist yours?' and right then a neighbor called. I knew right then—I knew in the pit of my stomach even before I picked up the call—that they were calling about James." I told her that's how I'd heard you died.

It was a Saturday afternoon in July. Almost a decade ago now. I got a text message before the call.

Whenever someone offered me a ride (to the next town, up the road, in the back of a horse trailer or a pickup truck or semi hauling fresh blue Louisiana crabs), I made it a point to look them in the eyes. Most of the time, kindliness and warmth greeted me, but sometimes there was no one looking back. You could see a ghost had taken up residence—a glint, a shine, a spark, a beyond-fullness—or else it was complete hollowness, emptiness, a void. Once, a glossy-eyed man offered me a ride along the Pend Oreille River in northern Idaho, and after only a few moments in the passenger seat I realized he was drunk. I watched, stupefied, as he crossed the double yellow line. A few days later, in eastern Washington, a man with wild eyes approached me after I had set up camp in a town park. I needed him to go away, to disappear, Please, man, leave me alone, but he stayed put. I had a small pocket knife that I used to cut up salami and apples, but it wouldn't have been much good for self-defense. I didn't carry a gun, because I wouldn't have known what to do with it.

I remember I traveled across the Bakken oil fields in the passenger seat of a white company pickup truck with a man from Utah—a drill well safety inspector who offered me a ride near Watford City, North Dakota. He had those rare, startlingly honest eyes you don't happen upon too often. I accepted his offer without hesitation. This roadway was the most dangerous yet. Too many oil trucks and big water trucks. Too many land drilling rigs and trucks hauling trailers. An endless stream of triplex pumps, blowout preventers, coil tubing units, hydraulic catwalks, fire-resistant booms, frac tanks, iron roughnecks, dozers, diggers, pup joints, and porta-potties constantly threatened to run me off the road. So I put my bicycle in the back of the man's truck and got in the cab. His face was deeply tanned and wrinkled, and he wore gray and green fire-retardant coveralls with RULON printed in cursive over his left breast pocket. A gas station Frito pie wrapped in a wad of tinfoil sat in his lap. Rulon was good at eating while driving, and he was a steady driver. Not a single stain on his shirt, I thought, and then we hit a bump in the road and the Frito pie got all over his pants. He laughed.

After a few minutes on the highway I asked him if he could show me how fracking worked, so he drove me to his company's drill site. It looked like an offshore rig towering above the sea, only the sea was dry and barren and thick with dust. Near the rig, we met a British man in red Halliburton coveralls whose face was covered in mud. He complained for a while about a family of local raccoons living behind one of the sleeping trailers at the rig. After the coveralled man walked away, Rulon and I drove around the site so I could take some pictures with my phone. He parked the truck, then told me that whenever he's up here in North Dakota, it's like he's dead. "Half my life is worse than death," he said. His voice was almost hoarse. "I just sit in this truck and wait for my hitch to end. My wife's back home living her dream, and I'm happy to support her and my twins, but there comes a time when I have to live my dream too."

He paused a long time.

"Sometimes I don't even want to go home. It's just dead time up here."

I watched a natural gas flare flicker in the wind.

"I've never said that out loud before. Half my life is worse than death."

His truck windows were rolled up because outside it smelled like heavy machinery, methane, trampled grassland, sour crude. It smelled like hell.

"Sometimes I just don't even see a reason to live anymore." He paused a long time. "I don't even see a reason to live. It's not like I'm depressed—I get up every day and get in my truck and drive around and do my job. I'm good at my job, it's not like I'm one of these guys who's depressed all the time and can't even get out of bed. I'm a working man. Lately, though—"

His hands were large and dusty and wrinkled, and his palms were covered in calluses, but his fingernails were almost perfect, like he had just sat down for a manicure.

"I don't know," he said. "Something's wrong." I asked what he thought it was and he said, "It's just dead time up here, I don't know how else to explain it. I feel like I'm rotting, like I'm wasting away." We sat in silence for a few minutes. "It's okay, though. It's not so bad." He put the truck into gear, and we drove around in silence for a while on the unmarked oil roads. When he spoke again, he told me they believed his wife had borderline personality disorder, and they'd been fighting since the twins were born, eight years ago. "A good day," he said, "is a single text in the morning from the wife." He said this was his third marriage and his third set of kids, and he couldn't get a divorce because then he'd lose everything again and "it'll destroy her and it'll destroy me and it'll destroy the twins and I don't want that," he said. "I don't know what to do. A couple years ago—you can't tell anyone this part, don't use my last name at least—a couple of years ago, I'm just lying there on the couch, relaxing, and the boys are across the room playing with their LEGOs, and she just comes in and starts wailing on me. Just hitting me, over and over and over again, and the boys are just in shock, watching it happen. Apparently, she thought I was hooking up with my oldest daughter—the one from my first marriage. Which is just ridiculous. It's a common kind of jealousy, I guess, but to me it just seems ridiculous that my wife would think something like that. And that she starts hitting me? I don't know. So eventually I get a handle on her and pin her down and tell her she's gotta stop or I'm calling the police and she starts crying and telling me that I can't do that, 'You can't call the police, they'll take away my boys,' and so I say, 'Well, you've gotta stop hitting me,' and she says, 'Okay, okay, anything you want, just don't call the police,' and as soon as I promise not to call the police, she starts wailing on me again. Right there in front of the boys. Just wailing on me. At that point I'm like, 'All right, that's it,' and I call the police. And they show up, God bless them, and arrest her, and then I've gotta go down to the police station and get all the charges dropped and, honestly, I don't think she's ever forgiven me for that. How messed up is that? That she attacks me and then for the last two years holds it against me that I called the police? I don't know," he said. "What do you think?"

Your father used to beat you. You told me he hit you with his hands and his belt, a coffee mug, one time it was a ream of printer paper— five hundred sheets wrapped in clear plastic with the manufacturer's logo set in green and blue. Your mom called 911, and then she called my mom and you came over to spend the night. I think my mom picked you up; I do not think you walked all the way to my house, though maybe you trekked through the woods behind your house and across the highway with a flashlight in hand. These days there's a traffic light where you would've crossed, but it wasn't there at the time. Everyone was surprised when they put it in a few years ago. That night you slept on the couch and I slept on the floor in the living room. You masturbated in your sleeping bag after you thought I'd fallen asleep. Otherwise, I don't remember the night too well.

I ate canned tuna fish and mayonnaise packets spread over torti-llas, plus three apples sliced up and covered in Nutella for dinner, outside a church and its cemetery on Brent Road near Barnesville, Georgia. After dark, I spread my bedroll on the grass. A blue 1990s Chevy truck pulled into the parking lot, and at first I thought it was someone coming to tell me to leave. I waved; the headlights dimmed. I asked the man in the truck if he thought it was all right to sleep there, at the church, and he said he didn't see why not. He had deep grooves across his face, not wrinkles but scars. Intrigued, I stood there speaking to him by the light of his dashboard. The cicadas were almost deafening, and his arms were so thoroughly tattooed that you could not see the skin underneath, especially with the moon as small as it was. He told me he was about to redeploy to Afghanistan.

I had read 104 degrees that afternoon on the gas station thermometer in Molena, Georgia, where the woman behind the cash register let me cool down for an hour in a refrigerated room full of ice-cold beer, but the summer air was almost cool that night as it breathed through the leaves. The man in the truck had a composition notebook in his lap. He told me he was writing a letter to his girlfriend before he shipped out. "I don't want to see her tonight," he said. "I don't want to worry her." I nodded. "She'll go out there and see it in her mailbox in the morning," he said. I wanted to ask him if I could read the note, but I didn't. His truck was still in the parking lot when I fell asleep; in the morning, he was gone.

I knocked on another truck window a couple days later. Or was it a couple months later? An air-conditioned government vehicle in Texas. It was parked on a dusty levee road alongside a twenty-six-foot rust-colored security fence. Security fence, as in border wall. Two uniformed soldiers—a young man and an even younger one—greeted me from behind tinted glass. Camouflage fatigues, body armor, a pistol strapped to each of their chests. Beyond the wall: thick brush and the Rio Grande.

I asked the soldier on the side of the truck closest to me what they were doing out here. He said, "What does it look like I'm doing? I'm sitting in this truck here, smoking cigarettes, drinking Monster, watching for illegals—that's it, man. I can't really talk about it more than that. What the fuck are *you* doing out here?"

The cold air blowing out his rolled-down window felt good. I tried to explain what had brought me to the Rio Grande on a bicycle, but couldn't find the right words. Then I asked how long they had been sitting here, and the same soldier said, "Four months." I asked him how long they would be staying, and the second soldier, the younger one, spoke up: "We have no fucking idea." To that, the older-looking soldier turned to him and said, "Man, we're under orders not to really discuss what we're doing. No photos, don't give out our name, none of any of that. That's what they told us, you know that." The second soldier said, "Let me talk, man." He'd arrived here, to his new post, only four days ago, from an army base somewhere, it didn't matter where, he said. "I'm not doing my job. I'm a combat medic. It's bullshit. For them, I'm just a warm body and a pair of eyes." He looked about my age, though with shorter hair and even more tired eyes. He had dropped out of college and joined the army to save lives, he said, and yet here he sat, in the Texas heat, talking to me until I left him alone.

Sugarcane, scrub brush, hundreds of monarch butterflies. My mind wandered as I rode through heat. Hundreds and hundreds of monarch butterflies flying I do not know where. Suddenly, we are eleven years old again, riding our bicycles down a big hill on Pecos after an afternoon at the neighborhood swimming pool. The sound of the wind, the sound of the trees, the sound of a fishing rod. Your laugh. I swore I could hear you laughing, yet when I looked over my right shoulder I was riding alone down a big hill toward the Rio Grande. Still, I felt more alive than the moon.

It was early October, more than a year into my travels, almost one hundred degrees at dusk, when I got the text saying another friend from middle school had died. I stood in a grocery store parking lot as I read that Jay Peterson was dead.

I booked a room at the La Quinta in McAllen, Texas, near the interstate. I needed to take a hot bath. Paradise takes many forms, and as it bubbled around me I thought about the sponge bath I had taken in the gas station sink not even a full day earlier. Antibacterial hand soap, paper towels, the clean metal sink. I thought about the man in black sandals on his way to pick up his dead sister's kids from elementary school. I still don't know why he told me she was dead. Or maybe I do, and what I don't know was the reason I stood there in the parking lot listening as he told me. The thought collapsed; the tub drained. I wept for his loss, though I had already forgotten his name.

I emerged from the soak, I checked my phone. I had received a few messages from a middle school crush:

Jay shot himself in a big open pasture next to a landfill in Austin.
It was where he liked to go when he wanted to be alone.
And his father found him the next day there.
It's so awful and terribly sad.
I'm gonna be speaking at his funeral and in my head I know everything to say but since he's gone I kinda don't know what to say except I fucking miss you and wish you knew how much I cared.

I remember trying to speak at your funeral. It felt like everyone we knew in the entire world was there. Old teachers, ex-girlfriends, friends from elementary school; your grandparents in the front row, mine somewhere near the back. I remember I wore my first suit, which I'd bought for the occasion at the Macy's in the Barton Creek Square Mall. I wonder if Jay was there. When I gave my eulogy, my voice shook as I told you goodbye.

* * *

I carried the weight of your death through midwestern soybean country, along the Missouri and Mississippi Rivers, through the southern pine forests and cotton fields, and up the hills they call mountains in New Hampshire and Maine. It was the constant preoccupation of the lonely voice at the back of my head. Why did you kill yourself? *Did* you kill yourself? Sometimes I wonder if maybe you didn't kill yourself at all. You couldn't have done it. Wouldn't have done it. You cared about me too much. And even if you didn't care, you knew you had to protect your sister. Maybe you were just a dumb kid who didn't look both ways before crossing a busy road.

On the Fourth of July I woke up at three thirty in the morning and rode down a busy highway in the dark. Around noon, I stumbled upon a parade in Turner, Maine, and as I was watching the fire trucks and tractors I thought about drowning myself in a lake called Mud Pond. I saw it on Google Maps a few miles up the road. One afternoon a few weeks later, after a long lunch with old friends in Manhattan, I thought about jumping onto the subway tracks.

Jumping in front of a train in New York; out the twenty-fifth-floor window of a friend's apartment building in Chicago; off a concrete bridge over the muddy Missouri River, flowing toward the Gulf Coast. I don't care to recall how serious I was about the idea. Still, I wonder if these thoughts are common. I asked a friend from California what he thought, and he wrote me an email:

I remember thinking about jumping in front of the school bus as it pulled away from the stop after dropping me off from middle school. I played the trombone in the band, and I pictured what my trombone would look like if a bus ran it over. It feels scary to write these things down. For me, those thoughts really are fleeting—not serious, not something I think I would ever carry out. I hope your thoughts are similarly transient, but if they aren't, I want you to tell me. We can make a mutual promise about it if you want.

A few days later, I swore to my friend on the telephone that I would never take my own life. The promise felt at once important and absurd. Then he asked what had stopped me from killing myself in New York. I told him that as the subway train screeched into the station, I received a call from a stranger with good news. His voice was what stopped me, I said.

I had lost my wallet a day earlier, in Brooklyn, and the man on the other end of the phone told me he'd seen it perched on top of a storm drain, looked me up online, found my number listed on Facebook, and called me: "Could you meet me right now?" Of course I could. I climbed the stairs up out of the subway station and walked in the rain through a park with benches and a fountain and then I descended into another subway station no more than half a mile from the first. A few minutes later, the man on the phone carried his own bicycle down the same stairs. I watched as he handed me the wallet, in slow motion, almost as if I weren't there.

We boarded the same uptown train and found ourselves discussing the weather, a tremendous summer storm. I do not understand people who do not enjoy talking about the weather, and felt glad to have a companion who also reveled in the awe of thunderclaps and hot raindrops among the city's trees. I never asked him his name, but he was a good listener, and before long I was telling him about the lonely voice, your suicide, was it a suicide, what was I doing traveling these roads? He waited for me to say more.

I looked down at my feet, and when I did not speak again he asked me to answer my own question, what was I doing still traveling these roads, though I suspected he knew I would say I was traveling because you'd never had the chance. I began this bicycle trip searching for America, I said, and even if I had found something like it, I wonder who else would have recognized what I said I'd found. Then I remembered a passage I had read in *Travels with Charley* a few weeks after setting off on my bicycle: "There are too many realities. What I set down here is true until someone else passes that way and rearranges the world in his own style." The man nodded in agreement. I started to say something else about the voice in my head, but the thought quickly unraveled into Steinbeck again: "...our morning eyes describe a different world than do our afternoon eyes, and surely our wearied evening eyes can report only a weary evening world." As the subway surfaced, water droplets spattering the train windows near 125th Street, my new friend told me he was also quite lonely and exhausted sometimes. That everyone has a voice in the back of their mind. "Some people hear it louder than others," he said with a laugh. I wondered if he was right. "You've gotta ignore about half the things your brain tells you sometimes. These feelings don't last forever; man, it'll be all right." That night, I closed my weary evening eyes, and when I opened them again it felt like morning. A miracle.

I was always looking to move. Always heading forward, onward, toward the next gas station conversation or little town set along a two-lane road. So when I met a man near Minot, North Dakota, who offered me a trip skyward, it felt natural to accept. His crew was working construction on a television broadcast tower, and he wanted to hoist me to the top of it with a skid winch and a gin pole, which is basically a crane and pulley system attached to the top of the tower that can haul up workers and gear. I did not hesitate—or at least I didn't hesitate for long—when he grabbed leather work gloves, a red construction helmet, and full-body harnesses from the toolbox in his truck bed. This was a rare chance to see North Dakota's flatness from above.

I received a quick safety briefing on fall protection as the skid winch's engine sputtered to life. Rory Kiland's feet left the ground a few seconds before mine. I was scared, and then I was weightless. The skid winch lifted us alongside the television broadcast tower, ten, fifty, one hundred feet off the ground: "You know, for us, some days we're up on these things and you might get a crop duster coming along and you can actually see into his cockpit." We were headed skyward, two hundred, three hundred, four hundred feet: "To the west there, you can see the wind. Which you never get to see—the wind in the grain fields. You don't think about it till you see it from up here!" When I looked straight down, I saw a group of toy trucks, his crew, watching us, and when I looked out toward the horizon, I saw blue lakes and green pastures, blacktop roads and wheat fields blowing in the wind. At eight hundred feet we stopped moving upward and just hung there for a little while, suspended from the television transmission tower by a five-eighths-inch wire rope. "Pretty cool, yeah?" Rory Kiland shouted into the wind. I don't recall exactly what I replied, but I think it was something like, This is crazy awesome.

Maybe two weeks later, I was finishing a cheeseburger at the only restaurant that wasn't a gas station in Fort Belknap Agency, in northeastern Montana, the tribal headquarters for a Nakoda and Aaniiih reservation by the same name, when a lanky young man walked through the door. Thomas Molina was wearing a cowboy hat as he ordered the chicken strip dinner, but he took it off when he sat down in the empty chair at my table. I had been traveling empty roads—thirty-two, forty-five, sixty-one miles between each conversation—and it was especially nice to have someone my age to talk with for a little while. I told him my name. He said he worked for the local suicide prevention group on the reservation. "We've lost eight people already this year." All to suicide, he said, including his best friend, and also his first cousin, who hanged himself in a closet when he was drunk. "That's the fourth of my brothers I've lost growing up here." Thomas paused. Not actual brothers, he said, so much as brothers in the way you were a brother to me. And then his chicken tenders arrived in a Styrofoam box, gravy in a little cup with a plastic lid, and he said, "Our ways, that's what'll save us, our ways—the sweetgrass, the pipe, the sweat lodge, that can save us. Our elders say addiction and drugs and poverty have become our ways, and our culture, but I think we need to change that." He spoke with enthusiasm: "We need to replace them with the old ways. That's what I'm working on." He picked up his hat from the table and walked out the door. I never saw him again.

I was still thinking about Thomas Molina's first cousin, the one who hanged himself while he was drunk, when I neared Browning, Montana, an outpost town on the Blackfeet Reservation. I had been traveling across the Great Plains for almost three weeks, and strong headwinds each day made riding the bicycle a slow and unpleasant affair: what normally would have been an eight-hour day in the saddle took twelve or sometimes fourteen hours while battling the wind. My saddle sores were infected, I wasn't eating enough, it was difficult to think over the sound of the wind. There was little else to do except ride. Then I saw the Rocky Mountains towering in the distance. It felt like spotting land after three weeks lost at sea.

Browning was a small town, though it had more than one main road and so it was large enough to get lost in. I asked a squat, balding man who was mowing the lawn in front of a chain-link fence for directions to the casino, where I had booked a room for the night. I needed to bathe and rest in a bed for a few nights before heading up Logan Pass. He told me to keep going down the street until it turned to the right, past a few trailer houses and a small bridge and some dogs. "They're probably harmless," he said. "Once you hit the main street, head west for three or four more blocks and you'll see it past the grocery store." I returned a few minutes later—when I did, the man said, "What's up, you get lost already?" and I told him I wasn't lost so much as lonely, man. Do you have a minute to talk? He turned off the lawn mower: "C'mon, c'mon, come sit down," he said. There was no sidewalk or curb; we sat in the dirt. He asked where I was from, and I told him, and he told me he was from here, right here. "We're Amskapi Piikani, Blackfeet blood," he said. He looked disappointed when I didn't recognize the name. "One of the most feared tribes ever, man. That's why everyone hates us." He laughed. "I'm not full-blood, but I'm half-full-blood." He pulled out a laminated identity card to prove it, listing a 41/64 blood quantum. "My mom was more." I asked if this house was his and he told me he was just here doing a job. "I'm sitting here doing yard jobs because I can't fucking get a job in this fucking dump," he said. There was an old speedboat sitting on cinder blocks in the front yard. "There's no fucking jobs." He said lawmakers had promised people resources and assistance, but had instead cut several government programs and started plans to frack the land. "I was a fireman for sixteen years. And look what I'm reduced to—you know? It's fucking dumb."

I asked him how he felt about it.

"I'm about ready to cry."

I reached for his shoulder, but pulled my hand back.

"I'm so mad. You know, all these guys want to do is fucking make money off us and fucking leave us in the dark. And what can you do?"

I didn't know what to say. He told me he'd lost his wife two years ago: "She got hit by a car, she died really bad."

I thought about you, brain-dead in the middle of a busy avenue, and I thought about what my body would look like if it were mangled in an automobile crash. I put the thoughts out of my mind and asked him to tell me something about his wife. He said, "Well, she came home and took me and said, 'Babe, come lay down by me. Hold me, I'll always be here.' I went to work, she went to work, and she showed me what love was. I never knew it because I grew up in a family that was very violent." He said he'd had to fight all this life. At three years old, his teachers tied bells on his shoes because he was always trying to escape school. "I was always going home to protect Mom."

He paused.

"I was about four years old—I used to hide in the weeds, me and my brother, about this high, and watch Dad yell out the door."

I asked, You remember it?

He said he remembered everything—fighting, protecting his mom, waking up in the morning to relatives passed out in the kitchen, stepping over people to get to the fridge. "Basically, we took care of ourselves." He taught himself to read and went to college and learned to jump out of helicopters to fight wildfires. "I just wanted to help people 'cause I was hurt so young." He lived well, bought a boat, a four-wheeler, and a house a few miles from town, in a place called Bear Paw. "I used to have a good name," he said. "I used to walk around this town and even old people would shake my hand. I didn't know them. People recognized me, you know, going to the store and whatnot, and I don't know how I fucking lost that."

He got a DUI and went to prison. He gave up his house to his sister and, after he got out, he went to eastern Washington to find a new job on a different reservation. It didn't work out. He said he had just gotten back a little while ago. "I don't know," he said. "There's a puzzle piece missing. Man, lately this world's been kicking my ass."

He laughed until he cried.

"I don't know what I'm trying to find, I don't know what the puzzle piece is."

He was crying so hard now that he wasn't making real words. It's okay, it's okay, I said before I put my arm around his shoulder for real this time. The back of his neck felt like my dad's after a sweaty afternoon in the garden. I did not know what else to say. He wasn't letting up. I scrambled for words: You know, I'm traveling around and all I'm trying to figure out is how to live a life, you know, it's so hard to live a life, just to live it, just to live the life, and then to be happy, is—

"I used to know all this shit. I took psychology, that didn't help me."

You feel without hope?

"I'm dead inside."

No, I said.

I paused. You don't mean that.

"Yeah, I do. I'm just wandering this world, wondering why God didn't take me."

How do you mean?

"Fucking end my life."

No, no, I said. I didn't know what to do.

"I'm going to be forty this year and it feels like I didn't do a damn goddamn thing in my life. I'm not proud of nothing. I did the world, but I'm not happy."

You saved a lot of lives, man, and it ripples. You know what I mean? You saved someone's life and it touches everyone. They might not know your name, but you did that.

"Of course I saved a lot of lives. It just don't matter anymore."

He was crying again.

"What am I good for?"

The words hung in the air for a while, and then he collected himself. We talked for a few more minutes, and he told me that he loved watching history programs on television and that he'd made varsity football as a freshman and that he'd met a *Gemini* astronaut once, the one who closed the hatch, and then a heavyset man with a mullet drove up in a diesel pickup truck and a woman with grass stains on her T-shirt hollered out the passenger window to him that it was time to go. "I'll be all right," he said. "I just hope you have good travels, and I'll pray for you." I said I'd love to stay in touch, and my new friend told me he didn't have a phone line connected, but he gave me his name and his Gmail address.

I wrote him an email that night. Still, I never heard from him again.

I do not know what happened. Did he kill himself? Did you kill yourself? Back home, in the last few years, Quentin overdosed, Spencer crashed his car into a trash truck, Jay shot himself in the head. We were fifteen years old when you died.

Hard-packed gravel roads and busy four-lane highways. Gas station, gravel pit, baseball field. At some point, in eastern Washington, a man in a blue T-shirt working in his front yard stuck out his hand to give me a high five. I lost eighty dollars gambling that afternoon. Then I rode over the Cascades and along the Columbia River to Cape Disappointment. The sight of the Pacific Ocean in Oregon brought tears to my eyes.

Church, campground, train station. I boarded a long-haul Amtrak in Los Angeles and spent two days eating kosher hot dogs in the train's observation car, watching the desert speed by through large, dirty windows. California, Arizona, New Mexico, almost home, Texas again: just me and my bicycle and the wind. A few days after disembarking the train, I saw a woman and a child sitting in folding canvas chairs among a grove of live oaks, their belongings piled in a large clear plastic bag. Beside them there was an orange ribbed ten-gallon water jug on a plastic folding table; two uniformed federal agents stood guard under a blue E-Z UP tent. The woman and the child sat shackled in the kind of chairs we always brought camping.

Did he kill himself? Should I kill myself? The words lived in my head like bees.

* * *

It went on like this for months, mile after mile through the fuck-you heat. Just keep pedaling, *Did he kill himself, you oughta kill yourself,* just keep pedaling all the way home. Eventually I stopped and sat down to rest near a pile of desert brush along a barbed wire fence outside Roma, Texas, until my vision swam. I had forgotten to refill my water bottles in the last town, and it was over one hundred degrees. I thought I was going to die there in the shadelessness. No wind, no clouds, no cars or trucks or even a US Customs and Border Protection surveillance blimp. No water, I needed water. I wondered what it would feel like to die, and then I laughed at myself, thinking about thinking about what it would feel like to die. I got up and started riding again. Just keep pedaling, man! I sang it as a song: Just keep pedaling, just keep pedaling, just keep pedaling all the way home. And then I hit the ground. I was on the ground, I left this world. No, I wasn't dead, thank god, I wasn't dead. So I got up, and a few miles later I knocked on the window of an armored US Border Patrol pickup truck parked in a brushy pullout, and without my having to ask, the driver handed me an ice-cold bottle of water from the cooler in the passenger seat. I downed it. He handed me another. I downed it. We might've made small talk as I drank the third bottle. I collected myself. He handed me a fourth bottle of water. It was also ice-cold, and my vision came back into focus as I said: How many years you been doing this?

"Five."

You were in the military?

"No, I just joined straight up."

Why's a guy like you join up?

"Oh, I don't know, thought it'd be exciting."

Any memories on the job come to mind?

"No, not really, I mean, sometimes I guess someone tells you something that sticks with you."

He paused.

"You know what I mean? Like, I'm always talking to the people

I pick up and asking them how it's been, how their journey's been. You know, just like talking to them the way we're talking now." Usually, he said, most of the stories are mundane, but "a man told me that his mother, wife, and three children died on the journey here. I asked him, 'Was it worth it?' and he told me, 'No, it wasn't worth it at all. Lord, of course it wasn't worth it. Nothing could be worth that.' His children died crossing the river on a raft. All three of his children. We picked them up right around here, if I remember right. Almost a year ago, a long time ago."

I asked him how he copes with hearing a story like that. He told me he doesn't really talk to anyone about anything that goes on at work. "Of course, there are the people they make available for us, I could talk to them, but no, I don't talk to anyone."

Not even your wife?

"No, not really, not about work, at least. I just sort of keep it all to myself."

What's that like?

"It just becomes normal. I like going to the gym, like, a lot. I guess that's how I cope with everything. Getting strong, going to the gym, that kind of thing."

So you don't talk to your wife about it at all?

"Not really, man."

Do you ever think about that story?

"Sometimes I do. Not a lot. It was a long time ago. But some-times I will think about—"

I waited for him to say more.

"I guess sometimes I get sad," he said, "but not for long."

An 18-wheeler honked as it passed us on the main road.

"These are good people. They're really good people crossing— they don't mean anyone any harm at all. They're not trying to hurt anyone, and I'm just doing my job. You know, enforcing the law. A lot of people think we hate these people, but they're no different than any of the rest of us. They're coming all the time. Earlier today, we caught two groups on the road; we didn't even have to go into the brush."

I was less than five hundred miles from home, only a week left in my journey, when I met a woman behind the counter at a gas station near New Falcon, Texas. She had blue eyes, a soft voice, and four children. I bought a Coke and she told me she had lost her second child a week before harvesting started. "We own potato trucks," she said. "And my husband had this accident with him—he was repairing parts of a truck and our son touched the belt, the one that dumps the potatoes off the truck, and he touched the belt and got caught into it." His name was Margarito Jr. He was eight when he died.

"Eight years old," she said. When we were eight years old we played kick the can, cops and robbers, and gin rummy in the old quarry, down the hill from where we went to elementary school. I remember one afternoon you tripped and fell and split open your lip. "Margarito died in North Dakota," she said. I thought about the wind. "You can survive in the heat, but there's no surviving a North Dakota winter without proper jackets and fuel," and so almost every year since she was seventeen years old, Myrthala Cantu said, she drove with her family to North Dakota in the spring to plant, harvest, and process potatoes until the weather turned ice-cold. "I don't like the winter," she said.

The door jingled; a customer walked in and asked for fifteen dollars on pump two. When we were alone again, I asked Myrthala what she remembered most about her son, and she told me she remembered he loved North Dakota. "He always asked us, when it was time for us to come back to Texas, 'Can we stay here, can we stay here,' and we said, 'Why,' and he said, 'Because I love my friends.' And we always said, 'We can't stay here for the winter, it's too expensive, we don't have the money to survive during the winter.'" What else? She said Margarito loved playing in the trees. "If one day you pass by Tappen," between

Bismarck and Jamestown, on Interstate 94, "you can stop and visit him." I said I would try, though I knew I never would. "There's a beautiful grave there," she said. "It's painted blue."

And then, five hundred miles later, the sun set red and orange on the final night of more than a year on the road. I rode from Fredericksburg through Johnson City and made camp at the state park named for the river you loved. Everything looked familiar: the pecan trees, the wooden picnic tables, even the asphalt ribbon leading from the limestone overlook to the campgrounds, near the river, nestled in a thicket of walnut, sycamore, and hackberry trees. One night, when I was sixteen, I snuck out and drove to the same overlook. There was a full moon that night, and the light it cast over the limestone made it feel like daytime. Naturally, I'd gotten a flat tire near a low-water crossing on the way home. I laughed at the memory; for dinner, I cooked my last box of macaroni, and I pulled out my headlamp to read.

There's a poem by a poet named Jack Gilbert that I'd been carrying with me in my saddlebags all these miles. Gilbert is writing about his late wife, Michiko, but whenever I recite his poem "Highlights and Interstices," I replace Michiko's name with the names I've heard and known. I read it to Myrthala, the woman I met at the gas station in New Falcon, Texas, only when I spoke it aloud I said "Margarito" instead of "Michiko." I would read the poem at your funeral if I could do it over again, but, you may remember, I recited a cliché instead, because when you died we were too young to say anything else. It occurred to me then, as I watched the moon rise near my campsite, that I might read the poem aloud, once more, before bed:

We think of lifetimes as mostly the exceptional
and sorrows. Marriage we remember as the children,

vacations, and emergencies. The uncommon parts.
But the best is often when nothing is happening.
The way a mother picks up the child almost without
noticing and carries her across Waller Street
while talking with the other woman. What if she
could keep all of that? Our lives happen between
the memorable. I have lost two thousand habitual
breakfasts with Michiko. What I miss most about
her is that commonplace I can no longer remember.

You know, we used to swim here, in the Pedernales River—
always a few weeks after a thunderstorm, once the water had cleared
up. One time, in high school, I remember, we had a picnic and ate
watermelon and Lay's potato chips and barbecued ribs. You climbed
way up into the canopy of a pecan tree and whooped and hollered to
the world below. No one had the courage to join you. You laughed;
we swam. I can't even recall who all was there. But now, at last, the
moon hangs over the river like I know it should.

A WORLD
WITHOUT
SELFIE STICKS

by ETGAR KERET

For Hamutal

IN RETROSPECT, I SHOULDN'T have yelled at Not-Debbie. Debbie herself always said that yelling doesn't solve anything. But what is a person supposed to do when a week after saying a tearful goodbye at the airport to his girlfriend, who was flying to Australia to do her doctorate, he bumps into her at an East Village Starbucks?

There she was, large as life, harassing the barista with questions about milk substitutes, and when I asked her how she could have come back to New York without even letting me know, she just gave me a cold look and said impatiently, "Mister, I don't know who you are. You must have me mixed up with someone else." That's when I lost it. After almost three years together, I'd hoped for more civil treatment. So when she said she didn't know me, instead of arguing, I stood in the middle of the Starbucks and yelled out all the intimate details I knew about her, including the scar on her back from when she fell on our trip to Yosemite and the hairy mole in her left armpit. Not-Debbie didn't reply, just gave me a shocked look as two café employees pushed me out.

I sat down on a bench on the sidewalk and started to cry. Five weeks earlier, when Debbie had told me she was moving to Australia, I'd been devastated, but I understood that the split was inevitable: the University of Sydney had offered her a doctoral grant, and I'd just been appointed to head a team at one of the hottest big data start-ups in the country. And, honestly, though the separation was painful, it wasn't cruel or humiliating, like that frigid encounter in Starbucks.

Suddenly, I felt a gentle touch on my shoulder, and when I looked up, I saw Not-Debbie standing next to me. "Let's be clear," she whispered. "I might look like her, with the mole and all, but I'm not her. Really!"

Not-Debbie and I moved to another café on Third Avenue. She ordered a weak cappuccino with a lot of foam, just like Debbie used to, gave me a searching look, also familiar to me, and began telling me the craziest story I'd ever heard. It seemed that Not-Debbie was also named Deborah, but she hadn't come to New York that morning from Australia. She'd come from a parallel world. I'm not kidding— that's what she said between sips of her weak cappuccino. She wasn't part of an alien invasion or the result of a scientific military experiment gone wrong. She was here as a contestant on a TV game show called *Vive la Difference*, the top-rated program in the alternate universe she'd come from.

Five participants on the show are sent to a universe that contains everything they have in their own world except for one thing, and that's what it's all about—figuring out what that one thing is that exists in their world but not in the one they've been sent to. The contestants are filmed 24-7, each on their own special channel, and the first one to discover what that missing item is and say it aloud is instantly returned to the TV studio in the world they came from, to the cheers of the audience and a million-dollar prize. And, to raise the stakes, while the winner celebrates, the other contestants have to live the rest of their lives in the alternate universe they've been sent to, never really knowing if they've lost the game or if it is still going on. This sounded to me like a hell of a price to pay for the losers, but Not-Debbie said it didn't bother her at all, because her ex was a real asshole, and she hadn't spoken to her parents in years.

It all felt too incredible to be a lie, and Not-Debbie spoke with such sincerity that I just had to believe her. Last season's winner, she said, was an immigrant from Ghana who discovered that in the alternate world the contestants had been sent to, the missing item was a selfie stick.

"A fucking selfie stick, can you believe it?" Not-Debbie said. "I would have never managed to figure it out."

I asked her a few more questions. It turned out that, like Debbie, Not-Debbie had studied clinical psychology, but she wasn't interested in being a therapist or getting a doctorate, which is why she now found herself stuck in an administrative job in some rich college in her alternate universe's upstate New York. I told her about my split from Debbie. About how I'd gone to the airport with her the week before and didn't leave the terminal until I saw her plane take off for Australia. She nodded and said it made sense. Contestants are never sent to the hemisphere where their parallels live, and if Debbie hadn't flown to Sydney, then she would probably have ended up in Buenos Aires or Auckland. "I'm glad she left," she said, giving me the smile that had made me fall in love with Debbie two and a half years ago. "With all due respect to Auckland, nothing beats New York."

When we finished our coffee, Not-Debbie insisted on paying, and right before we were about to go our separate ways, I offered to help her win the prize on the show. In order to find what her world had that ours didn't, Not-Debbie had to be exposed to as much information as possible, as quickly as possible, and I, as a computer person with expertise in databases, could help. When I saw her hesitate, I backtracked quickly and said that if helping her or using computers was against the rules of the program, then... But Not-Debbie smiled and interrupted me.

"It's not that," she said. "I just don't want to drag you into this whole complicated business. It's not like I'm just a girl you've never met before."

I explained that there was nothing complicated about it. Even though I'd been with Debbie for two and a half years, she was Not-Debbie and we'd just met today, and if it was okay, I'd be glad to help her look for the missing thing. And, who knows, maybe in the process, I'd become a TV star in an alternate universe.

At four in the morning, after nine straight hours of searching the technological, geographic, and culinary databases (would you believe that in the show's first season the parallel world was a world without maple syrup?), Not-Debbie said she couldn't keep her eyes open anymore. I changed the sheets on the bed in my small studio apartment for her and she fell asleep instantly. I sat and watched Not-Debbie sleep. It was weird, but I felt that in those nine hours I'd learned more about her than I'd ever known about my Debbie in the entire two and something years we'd lived together. The possibilities she'd raised in our search for the missing element had revealed so much about her dreams, her desires, her fears. It wasn't that she didn't resemble Debbie, but there was something else about her: she was open, brave, mesmerizing, and wild. I don't really know what to call it when it happens with someone who is both your ex and someone you've never met, but I fell in love. And while Not-Debbie slept in my apartment, so close I could smell her shampoo, I pictured the other four contestants on the show still searching for flying cats, electric ear cleaners, eyebrow deodorants, or whatever it was that was missing in this imperfect world. And I knew that all it took for Not-Debbie to stay here with me forever was for one of them to find it. I closed my eyes.

When Not-Debbie woke me at one in the afternoon, she seemed a little slower. She told me it had taken an average of fifteen hours for winners from previous seasons to find the missing element, and she'd been searching for more than a day already. "That's it," she said. "One of the others must have found it already."

I tried to reassure her. After all, there was no way of knowing—maybe they were baffled, wandering around Manhattan or wherever they'd been sent, and she could still win. "Maybe," Not-Debbie said, suddenly smiling, "but the truth is that from the minute I went on the program, I've been fantasizing about losing and starting a new life in this world—a better, less painful life than the one I had back home."

I didn't say anything, and she looked at me softly, in a way Debbie had never looked at me. "Honestly?" she said, and touched my face with the back of her hand. "Who cares what's missing in this world? You're here."

In bed, when I asked her if she was on birth control, she shook her head and said with a smile that she really hoped that of all the possible parallel worlds, she hadn't landed in one without condoms. It was a joke, but when she said it, I could see her hesitate for a second out of fear that maybe it was true, and that saying it aloud would return her to her world and separate us forever. After the sex, when I suggested we check out the astronomy, geopolitics, and history databases, she said she'd rather have sex again.

Later, we went for a walk in Central Park and ate hot dogs. Not-Debbie told me that in her world she's a vegetarian for reasons of conscience, but she feels that here in this world, which isn't her own, it's okay for her to eat a hot dog. "I don't want to win," she said as we stood by the lake. "I don't want to go back. I want to be here, with you." We spent the rest of the day in the city, showing each other our favorite places in Manhattan.

That's how we arrived at Trinity Church. It was already evening and the illuminated church looked enchanted, more like a palace in a Disney movie than a real place. I told her I'd passed it by accident ten years ago. I had just arrived in the city, and when I saw it, I swore that if I ever got married I'd do it there. Not-Debbie laughed and said being sure about the church was good; now all I had to do was find a girl who'd agree to marry me in it. I smiled, too, and right after we kissed, Not-Debbie said, "Let's go inside. I'm dying to see the place we're getting married."

The church was fairly empty, and from the minute we walked in, Not-Debbie kept looking around uneasily. I asked her if everything was all right, and she said yes, she was just looking for something. When I asked her what, she looked at me as if I were an idiot and said, "God." Then she added, "This is a church, right?" I nodded, and she said, "So he'll probably be back in a minute." I tried to calm her down. I said that I personally didn't believe in God, but even the people who do say you can't see him.

Not-Debbie shook her head slowly and said, "Wow, that's it! In your world, there are churches and mosques and synagogues, exactly like in mine, only there's not really a God in it. Don't you get it? It's a world without Go—" She didn't manage to finish that sentence, at least not in my world.

Six years have passed since then, and I still try to imagine what happened to Not-Debbie, how she arrived at the flashy studio and was welcomed with cheers from the audience and compliments from a pair of sleek presenters, who told her she had won a million dollars. Sometimes when I imagine it, she's happy, and tears of joy run down her face, but most of the time she's sad, searching the studio, looking for and not finding me. My heart might want to picture her happy, but my ego—my ego insists on believing that the day we spent together was as meaningful to her as it was to me. Less than a year after she slipped through my fingers, I married Debbie in Trinity Church. Life in Sydney wasn't for her, and two months after she returned to the city, we made a spur-of-the-moment decision. Sex with her, by the way, is never as spectacular as it was with Not-Debbie, but it's pleasant enough, and familiar, and we have two adorable, beautiful children, Zack and Deborah Jr., who will have to learn to live, as we did, in a godless world.

— *Translated by Sondra Silverston*

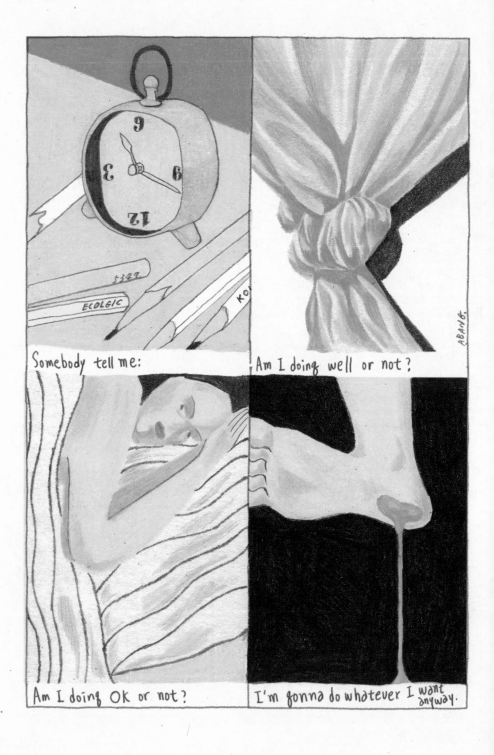

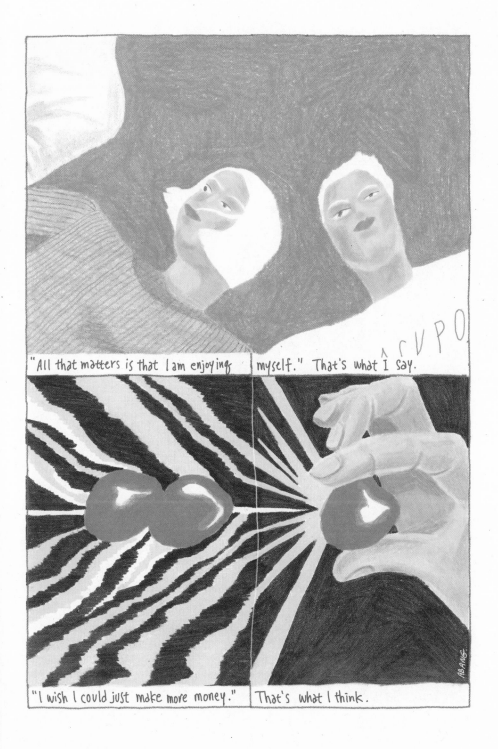

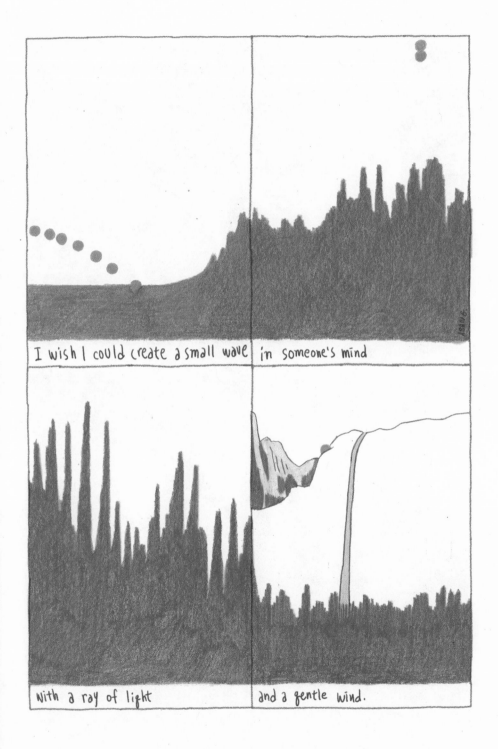

Damn.

I hide under the blankets when I get home.

And cry.

Why do I pretend to be strong?

A first : something I want to relive.

Something I want to forget.

Something vivid and alive.

Something I can't remember.

Why do I try to give so much? In the warm sun,

in the summer breeze, an ennui that drives you crazy.

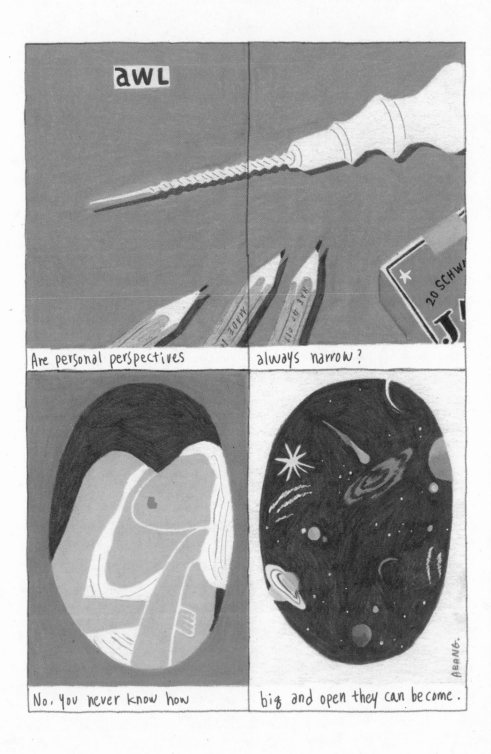

There're so many things I want to say.

But words fail me.

There are so many things to say

Without saying anything.

Too many egos.

Too many roles.

Someone can't be defined in just one way. Right?

EBBING'S CURSED TOCCATA

by RITA CHANG-EPPIG

WHEN LINUS FOUND THE yellowed sheets of music curled up like fetuses in the church where he played the organ, he immediately understood that his life was about to change. Every classical organist knew the story of Lucian Ebbing's cursed toccata, or at least a variation on its theme (Linus himself had heard at least three). Ebbing, having composed many acclaimed pieces in the early 1800s, such as Fugue in B Minor and *Fou de chagrin*, secluded himself in his final years to perfect his magnum opus. Speaking to no one except, rarely, the husband-and-wife groundskeepers of the church that housed his favorite pipe organ, Ebbing worked only at night, pushing and pulling stops, pawing insistently at the pedalboard. One night, as the groundskeepers got ready for bed, they felt a sudden foreboding. Neither could explain it to the other, but both knew, through the stuttering in their chests and the clenching in their bowels, that something was wrong. The two awoke the following morning to find dead starlings strewn all over the grass outside the church. Ebbing was slumped lifeless over the organ keys, with no visible wounds except for the blood trailing out of one nostril and down the staircase of the seven manuals before disappearing through cracks into the depths of the console. The lone copy of the sheet music, deemed too dangerous to be performed, was hidden away somewhere and quickly became lost to time.

Curse or no curse, how was a struggling musician to resist the temptation? Linus locked the door to the storage room and plopped down on a dusty trunk. Gaze lilting over the wide-ranging chords, the descending scale of the signature from capital E to long-tailed g, he experienced a sense of purpose for the first time in his twenty-two years of life: he was going to learn to perform this piece, or he was going to die trying.

Linus had been playing for long enough that, when approaching a new piece, he could hear the melody in his head while reading the score. This was by no means to suggest that he was a genius. Most musicians who'd received his level of training—private lessons throughout adolescence followed by four years in the conserva-tory—could do so comfortably. He had an earthly, not a heavenly or, for that matter, infernal talent. He always thought he'd have turned out better if not for the slight palsy in his left arm, acquired during the same accident that had killed his mother four years ago. As things stood, he was capable enough to get a job playing the organ at a suburban church every Sunday but not a position in an orchestra.

But when Linus sat down at his kitchen table with the score that evening, having taken the music home without informing anyone at the church of his discovery, he realized that he couldn't hear the music, at least not in full. Ebbing had written his final toccata for organs with pipes that sounded two octaves lower than the lowest C on the piano, lower than the human ear could perceive. Perhaps the church where Ebbing died had possessed such an oddity, but nowadays, most organs were caged within five octaves.

That didn't stop Linus from trying his hand at the piece. The next evening, he sat down at the console after the church had closed. His girlfriend, Savannah, perched herself at the very edge of the bench, her lower body twisted away from the pedals so as not to interfere with his feet. She loved to hear him play and told him so frequently. Said his music connected her to something unfathomable. She also frequently told him she loved *him*, though he felt less certain how to respond to that. The future seemed as unreal to him as the past few years of his life did: there had been the accident; then the hospital, with its phantasmagoria of interns and residents; followed by the rehab clinic, thick with the smell of broken bodies, and the clinic decorated entirely in green foam, or perhaps those two clinics had been one and the same and he was merely misremembering; and finally the conservatory, where he spent years locked in the practice room by himself, staring at the three five-octave manuals as though they were too-tall steps. Sometimes he stayed overnight at the school, experimenting with the Vox Humana stop to make the organ wail. It wasn't like he had any family members left to check in on him, and it certainly wasn't like he looked forward to sleep, what with the nightmares since the accident.

Taking a deep breath, Linus began to play.

The toccata was divided roughly into halves. The first half twittered to the top of the instrument's range, like cranes folded with increasingly small slips of silver paper. The second half slunk to the bottom, past the organ's range. Full of fast, lightly fingered passages, the toccata demanded far more of Linus than the hymns he'd grown used to since starting this job. His hands cramped as he continued. Next to him, Savannah swayed.

He crossed the midpoint. The tempo was slower here, the tone from the Contraposaune stop dry and hard. Savannah stopped swaying.

The pain in Linus's hands felt almost intolerable now, full-blooded, as if his heart were trying to push his life out through his fingertips.

The tempo hastened again near the final passage. Broken chords, amputating one another's extremities, collided, hurtling clumsily, clatteringly to the bottom. Linus watched, filled with an odd, disembodied horror, as his hand closed in on the barrier at the left edge of the manual. They were coming, the lowest notes. He couldn't play them, at least not on this organ, yet he couldn't seem to...

"Stop!" Savannah yelled. Then, with surprising strength, she shoved him off the bench.

He gaped up at her.

She seemed surprised at her own actions. "Sorry, I don't... I just felt scared all of a sudden. I told you to stop, but you didn't hear me."

"You felt scared?"

Later, as they sprawled on her couch, the remains of takeout littering the coffee table, she said, "So where did you say you got this piece of music? It doesn't seem like the kind of stuff the church asks you to play."

"It's for me," Linus said.

"But where did you get it? It looks, you know. Old."

Given the toccata's history and everything he knew about Savannah, he decided in favor of vagueness. "It turned up while I was looking for a tuning knife. I thought it'd be a good challenge."

Savannah seemed to be weighing her words. "Well, I don't like it," she said.

"You don't like it."

"The first part is nice, but then it gets weird."

"It gets weird."

"Look, I'm not a musician. I don't know how to describe this stuff. Maybe you should work on something else."

Linus hummed noncommittally, a sound she must have mistaken for agreement because she settled back into his arms. Earlier, at the church, Savannah had described a sudden fear. Linus himself hadn't noticed much outside of the pain in his hands, but now that he thought about it, hadn't he, too, felt some unease as he'd neared the end? It was probably the tritones in the second half, all the restless, dissonant chords. "The devil's interval," superstitious folks called this particular arrangement of tones, the same found in ambulance sirens. Music theorists described the feeling of listening to tritones as walking on a staircase that was missing its final step: these chords left you seeking a closure that never came. Or maybe his disquiet was from the steep descent to the lowest frequencies, the threat of deception, of something felt but not heard or seen, like the fleeting touch of a cold, unidentified object in the dark.

To make matters more complicated, Savannah was a true believer. She believed in all things a person could believe in and then threw in a few extras, just in case there was a quiz. There on the mantel was her altar to her guardian angel, the centerpiece a mauve-and-periwinkle watercolor of a cherub she had painted herself. On her bookshelf, in an overwrought wooden box, her moonstone runes nested like eggs. Her hair always smelled like sage. Feelings were not just feelings for her but omens. He hadn't mentioned to her the toccata's supposed history, but she might have taken one look at the crumbling yellow paper and heard the aberrant chords and jumped to her own conclusions.

Linus himself was undecided about whether anything at all existed beyond the tangible. The first couple of years after the accident, he'd refused to enter churches, a conviction that bewildered and infuriated his teacher, who once yelled at him during a particularly unfruitful lesson, "I don't care if you worship the Dark Lord himself. If you want to be a professional organist, you're going to have to play in churches."

A few months after that lesson, as he was passing the church on the way to the conservatory, he noticed that an old homeless woman had set up her bedroll in front of the building's chained iron doors. It had been a chilly morning, fall dipping a toe into winter to acclimate itself. She slept as if she were dead, or—and this thought didn't escape him—perhaps she already was. The sight filled Linus with what others might have mistaken for rage, except rage required a wellspring of feeling, some hidden aquifer of chemicals that had long ago dried out in him. *What a joke*, he mentally spit at the apostles framing the doors. *One would have to be an idiot to believe in you.*

At that moment, something blew past him, so close he felt it against his ear. It banged against the iron doors and collapsed on the front steps. The homeless woman woke, screaming. Breath bated, Linus approached the dark shape: a raven with its wings spread, its eyes like burned-out suns.

The following week Linus applied for and received a job as the backup organist of that church.

Increased familiarity with the piece brought only increased frustration. Linus had never experienced this himself, but he'd heard other people talk about it, the sting as though one's lover were hiding a secret. He was angry at it for withholding itself, angry at himself for not being worthy of it. Still, he remained entranced by the piece—when he played it, he felt the music spread through all his capillaries as if he were a puppet and it the warm hand animating him. That was, until he reached the unplayable part of the score. Extra time at the church, time snuck from Savannah, showed him only that he would never be able to fully know the toccata, that there would forever remain a divide between him and it unless he did something different.

And of course he had to think about his career. This song, on the right organ, could be his big break.

Arriving at the decision to move was easy enough. To play the piece properly, he had no choice but to travel to the Midwest, to one of the few places in the country with an organ that size. He would have flown to Europe to play at the church where Ebbing died, but that building had been destroyed in one of the world wars. Sometimes Linus had nightmares about those beautiful pipes splintering apart, the metacarpals and tibiae torn from the console core and scattered in the dirt.

Arriving at a decision about Savannah was far more difficult. Long-distance relationships hardly ever worked, he knew that. But Linus's mother, who'd been a friend of Savannah's aunt, had really liked Savannah, had even tried to set the two of them up on a blind date multiple times before they ultimately got together.

"So what are you saying?" Savannah asked.

He shrugged. He didn't know what he was saying.

"But we're doing so well. At least I think we are. It'd be such a waste to end it over something like this."

He picked at a hangnail. She chained her arms around him and exhaled warmly onto his neck. "Well, it's not *that* far away," she continued. "Maybe I can even get transferred to my company's midwestern branch. They might be able to use another person in HR."

It wouldn't be so bad to stay together, Linus found himself thinking. She grounded him, tethered him to reality. On days when he got too absorbed in practice, she reminded him to eat and take breaks. One could do a lot worse than make one's place in the world with such a woman. Yet he also couldn't deny the tremolo of anxiety inside. Her arms felt tight around his waist.

Three weeks later, Linus stepped off a bus a thousand miles away, all his belongings slung across his shoulders in two large duffels. He texted Savannah that he had arrived. *lmk when u can tlk*, she texted back, in her characteristically hard-to-decipher combination of abbreviations and misspellings.

He had rented an efficiency apartment, which he swung by for just long enough to dump his bags, shower, and dress in his only suit, the itchy polyester two-piece he'd worn to his mother's funeral. Résumé in hand, he hopped a bus to the cathedral he'd read about online. Built in the early 1900s, the church, at its height, had served more than four thousand families. But an economic downturn in the region some decades later had driven away most of the congregation. These days, the building was on the brink of closure. Linus's proposal was simple: In exchange for letting him play its now-neglected organ, he would help the church grow its influence again by putting on free concerts, offering free lessons, the works. He would go door to door, begging people to come to Mass, if that was what it took for him to lay his hands on that magnificent instrument.

Linus got off the bus and gaped at the massive structure before him. Built in imitation Romanesque style, the church crouched in wait, wide and heavy. Opening the wrought iron doors, he was momentarily stunned by a draft of hot air smelling of snuffed wicks and wood polish. "Hello?" he asked the space, trying to will his eyes to adjust to the darkness.

He moved deeper into the building, gliding his left hand along the tops of the pews so as not to bump into what seemed to be an excess of statuary, even for a cathedral. Slowly, his eyes began to pick out the details in the nave: tall pitchfork candelabras, green and white floor tiles laid in a vaguely reptilian pattern. What he had mistaken for statues turned out to be high-relief friezes depicting choirs of angels with hollow gray stares. Late-afternoon sun bled through ceiling windows tiny as thorn pricks.

Yes, there, above him. Each rank of the gleaming organ arranged first by increasing and then by decreasing pipe length, rising and falling like a final, silvery breath.

"May I help you?" a voice said from behind Linus.

Linus turned quickly, dizzying himself a little as he did so. Ever since the accident, his balance had been off. "Ah," he said to a dark-suited man. "I was wondering who I should talk to about the organ here. I'm an organist, and I'd like to offer my services to the church for free."

"Is that so?"

The man came closer. He was shorter than he had looked from a distance, with a sharp widow's peak that gave the impression of a single talon. His white collar suggested an affiliation with the cathedral.

Linus handed him his résumé, the paper trembling in his hand. "I think you'll see I've received the best musical education. And I have a lot of experience playing for churches." He recited his proposal as he'd practiced it in the mirror.

"Why here?" the man asked after glancing at the résumé. "Pardon my curiosity. I am, of course, very grateful that you want to volunteer your time here. But surely there are plenty of places a young man with your skill could play."

That question Linus hadn't prepared for. Feeling the seconds pass and cowed by the man's gaze, Linus opted for the truth. "I need a seven-octave organ for a piece I've been working on."

"I see." The man began walking toward the back of the church, gesturing for Linus to follow. "I'm Reverend Auguste Peters, the rector here," he said as the two of them climbed a creaky spiral staircase to the balcony overlooking the nave, the giant stone baptismal font bottomless in the low light. "The final decision lies with me. But first"—they turned a corner, and the massive wood console splayed its dark wings before Linus—"I want to hear you play."

Carefully, Linus sat down on the bench. The console had seen better days. No one had cleaned it in months, if not years. The tobacco-stain-colored keys gnashed together crookedly. Remnants of oil and skin from previous players gunked the cracks. A few of the stops were so worn he couldn't read the names anymore—he would have to figure out which ones they were by ear. "What do you want me to play?" he asked.

"This piece you've been working on," the rector said.

"I don't have the score with me."

"Whatever you remember is fine. I just want to get a sense of what kind of music might have possessed you to move hither from so far away."

Sliding off his shoes—street shoes on well-maintained pedals were bad enough, and these pedals looked about ready to break off—Linus tested a few notes, his socked toes doing their best to grip onto the organ's. Feeling suddenly self-conscious, he tested a few of the nameless stops. This one had to be Nachthorn. That one, Voix Céleste.

The anxiety dissipated as he played. Ask any musician and they'll tell you the anticipation is the worst part of a performance, the uncertainty of everything to come. The first half Linus had almost completely memorized. Up, up, lighter, faster. The Aeoline warbled thinly in the cavernous space.

Now, then, the second half. There was a run here, maybe, followed in quick succession by a fugal interlude, or was it the other way around? Sweat gathered along Linus's brow and above his lips, dripping onto the instrument as he muscled away at the pedals and manuals. His head ached.

"You can stop there," the rector said, placing a warm hand on Linus's shoulder.

"I'm sorry I don't remember the whole thing," Linus said.

"Quite all right." The man seemed oddly pleased. His wide smile jarred with his overall pallor and sharp countenance. "It has been a long time since I last heard this song."

"That's not possible," Linus said, too tired to get into the story of the toccata. "This piece is... new. It's by a new composer."

"Is that so?" The rector clapped loudly, startling Linus. "You will have to fix up the organ yourself, of course. We lack the money to hire someone. The pipes like enough need cleaning. Other parts may need to be repaired for you to play the song as you should."

They shook on this: a pact. Reverend Peters ("Call me Auguste," he insisted) even went so far as to give Linus a copy of the keys. "Feel free to come practice whenever you wish," he said. "I verily believe the music finds the musician, and this music has clearly found something inside you. Who knows? You might be just the revelation this congregation needs."

Linus settled into his new routine without much trouble. Shortly after dawn every day, he set out for the cathedral, black coffee in his thermos and a protein bar in his pocket. Auguste's only request had been that Linus not practice or maintain the organ during times when people were likely to come for worship. Hardly an issue, as the church was usually empty, but Linus obliged by reading up on organ repair during Mass and Communion. After morning Mass, he got to work replacing keys and cleaning pipes, though he learned the dangers of his own hubris after nearly falling to his death trying to disassemble one of the longer pipes, the longest of which measured sixty-four feet. To clean those he would have to dig deep into the payout from his mother's life insurance and hire a professional.

Linus didn't know how he felt about Auguste. Certainly, Linus was thankful, but he'd have been lying if he said he wasn't also a little unsettled by him, by the way the man always seemed to float just out of sight. Whenever Linus felt hopeless, or found himself questioning his decision to move here, Auguste materialized with words of encouragement. The other day, after many failed attempts at a run, Linus gathered his things to leave. Auguste appeared at the bottom of the stairs right as Linus neared the top. "You are leaving particularly early," Auguste said.

"It's just not going to happen today," Linus said. "I might go home and take a nap."

"Is that wise?"

"What do you mean?"

"I mean," Auguste said, not moving from his place, "that not even God rested until he had completed his task."

Linus laughed nervously. "Is it wise to compare me to God?"

"I suppose I am just so overcome by your talent that I fear you will succumb to the demons of self-doubt. You can always rest here. I shall fetch a blanket." Linus found Auguste's insistence strange but didn't feel comfortable arguing. To Linus's surprise, after a nap on one of the pews, he mastered the run.

"You act weird when you have to deal with older dudes," Savannah had once said, not incorrectly. Linus had never known his father, but then, neither had his mother. She'd gone to a sperm bank after decades of unfruitful prayer for a good man. As a child sitting in Mass every Sunday, Linus had imagined his father to be more than human, a being that dwelt high in the sky or deep in the earth, unreachable except in death.

On a few occasions, homeless men and women wandered through the doors. Auguste received them with kindness, even offered to connect them to city services. Yet they never stayed long. Once, a man lay down on one of the pews to nap. Scarcely more than a half hour later, he awoke screaming and crashed out of the building, leaving behind a plastic bag full of what appeared to be birdseed. Another time a woman who spoke an Eastern European language begged Auguste for a favor, literally falling to her knees in front of him as she cried. Auguste, who apparently also spoke the language, laid his hand on her shoulder. The woman looked up at the rector with a shocked expression, crossed herself twice, and stumbled back out into the cold.

In the evenings, Linus practiced, doing his best to avoid the pipes that still needed cleaning. Sometimes Auguste stayed behind to listen, that same satisfied look on his face, though the expression seemed also tinged with nostalgia, like he really had heard the piece before Linus showed up. In this way, Linus easily fell back into habits from his conservatory days. The Vox Humana kept him company in the amniotic darkness, like a child's conversation with himself on his way to the bathroom at night. Down on the main level, the saints and apostles cast long shadows in the candlelight, as though dragging wayward souls behind them.

Occasionally he remembered to text Savannah. She was understandably not happy about this negligence, so sometimes she called him, yelling. Late one night, after he'd scratched his forearm trying to dislodge a bird's nest from inside one of the ranks, Linus yelled back, though he regretted doing so immediately. She was simply worried about him. She was the only person left in his life who worried about him. He began to apologize, spouting lies about the new rector and his unreasonable demands, when suddenly he heard a gasp. "You're playing that song, aren't you? The old one," Savannah said. His silence was answer enough. "You said you wouldn't play it anymore!"

"It's just a song," he said.

"I've been thinking about it since that time," she said. "It wasn't just me being sensitive."

He wasn't surprised by her unease. He'd been thinking about the music, too, upon rising and also when lying down; during meals, while staring into the stone cherubs' mold-rimmed eyes; in trances when the toccata played for him, denuding and bisecting itself before him, peeling back the edges of its own skin to reveal... what? That was usually the point when he returned to his senses. But all that thinking helped him understand that there was, indeed, something about the music that conjured demons—psychological ones, at least. His nightmares had definitely grown more frequent. He was even having ones he hadn't had since immediately after the accident. Rarely did a morning find him well rested.

She was just reacting to the tritones, he explained. Still, he promised to text more. She promised to keep an open mind about the music. They nodded off to the sound of each other's breaths.

The first few months after the accident, Linus had often had dreams in which he was climbing either up or down a long staircase but could not reach the end. Once, a grizzled woodsman with a shotgun slung across his back barred him from the top. Behind him sprawled a deep forest—frenzied chirping revealed that the leaves on the trees were in fact birds. "No one is invited a second time," the man said. Another time a beautiful woman dressed all in dark, liquid red appeared before him. On her left shoulder perched a bird. Suddenly the bird pecked through the woman's breast, into her heart, and began drinking from her; soon she was no more than a trickle on the ground. The bird flew away.

For a while he wondered if the dreams were trying to tell him something. It didn't seem wholly impossible. On the day of the accident, the nightmare world had punctured the waking one. This reality gaped open and bled out into another.

"You flail in your sleep," Savannah had told him a few weeks after he'd started spending the night.

"What?"

She tugged her collar aside to show a bruise dawning over her clavicle.

"Oh my god," he said, horrified.

"What I put up with because I like you," she said, clearly joking, but he didn't laugh.

"Maybe I should stop staying over," he said.

"Don't be silly," she said. "I'll just glom onto you like a sea monster when we sleep, so you can't move your limbs."

She hadn't shown him another bruise since then, nor did he find one, though he couldn't shake the suspicion that she'd just gotten better at hiding them.

*   *   *

The professional cleaners came, removed the longest pipes, and promised to return with them soon. Which worked out as far as the timing was concerned because Savannah was in town. It would be their first time seeing each other in more than three months.

Linus gave her a tour of the church. She seemed quieter than usual, but her face was hard to read in the dim. His heart pattered as they climbed the iron staircase.

"Oh," she said when she saw the console.

Without pressing down, she stroked a finger horizontally across the keys as if along vertebrae, as if afraid of waking a wild animal. The church was so quiet that Linus could hear her breathing, fast and shallow. The sound of a throat being cleared made the two of them jump.

"You're still here," Linus said, turning to find the rector a few feet away. It occurred to him briefly that Auguste moved like one of the church's many statues, which was to say that he didn't seem to move at all. Rather, he was ever-present, and people either took notice of him or not. "Sorry, I thought you'd gone home for the day."

"Pray tell, who is this lovely young woman?" Auguste asked.

Linus introduced the two. Auguste lifted Savannah's fingertips as if to kiss them but merely kept her hand aloft, the way one might hold up wares in a marketplace to examine them, until she withdrew it. "I have big plans for Linus," Auguste said. "His music is the syringe wherewith we will add new blood to this diocese."

"I'll try my best," Linus said.

"You will," Auguste said.

The rector excused himself. Linus had been about to sit down on the bench when Savannah said, "Let's go back. I'm beat."

"Do you want to hear—" Linus began.

"Now. Please."

They rode home in silence. Linus would have guessed she was

mad at him about something, except that the moment they entered his apartment, she molded her body around his like a caul. "I love you," she said. "I want you to be happy."

"I want you to be happy too," he said.

He wished she would stop waiting for him to repeat the first part. What he offered wasn't close to what she deserved, but then this whole relationship had been her idea from the start.

She'd come to one of his recitals during conservatory in search of free food: it was common knowledge among locals that student recitals were generally well catered (but almost never packed), and if one had the time, one could emerge from the two hours with a full stomach and perhaps even a sense of having been entertained. Linus's senior recital had been especially empty, attended only by his teacher and a few fellow organists. Instead of leaving as soon as the lights came on, Savannah stayed to talk to him. She wore five different rings on five different fingers—raw turquoises and citrines and the like, whatever had the best "vibes"—but still there was a certain grace to the way she extended her hand with her head tilted slightly, the line from her cheek to her neck to her shoulder like a treble clef. He didn't realize who she was until their first date, when she finally admitted their connection. It felt as if his mother were making one final plea. *Look, Squirrel, just do this for me, okay?*

He was clear about his situation from the start: the nightmares, the bouts of depression, his utter lack of interest in starting a family. Somehow those deficiencies made Savannah like him more. He'd reminded her that, as a musician, he would more than likely have to move many times before being able to settle down. She'd always dreamed of traveling, she said. In retrospect, maybe some part of him had hoped that by divulging all this she would be the one to end it.

At least he'd warned her, he told himself whenever the guilt sidled too close. At least he'd gotten the words out.

* * *

"You're humming in your sleep," Savannah said about a week into her visit. "That song. And you got out of bed the other night and just stood in the middle of the room. I think you were sleepwalking."

"Maybe it's stress?" Linus said.

As the repairs on the organ neared an end, he had begun to provide community outreach, a task for which he proved eminently unqualified, what with his shyness and the years of self-imposed isolation in conservatory. But of course he'd neglected to consider that when he'd pleaded his case to the rector. Linus had spent the past week leaving at daybreak to hang up flyers and knock on doors, riding around the city on cold, sputtering buses. There were times he found himself having arrived at his destination without any awareness of how he'd gotten there, and other times he could have sworn he'd already arrived, only to remember he was still waiting for the bus. Once or twice he returned to the church instead of to his apartment as he'd intended, reeled in.

Meanwhile, the pipes were coming back one by one, each a silver needle pricking at the sky as if to bleed heaven. That afternoon, as Linus was overseeing the reassembly of the final pipes, Auguste sat down next to him and passed him a glass of red liquid.

Linus sniffed it. "Is this communion wine? I don't know how I feel about receiving the blood of Christ on a Thursday right before practice," he said jokingly.

"Unconsecrated communion wine is just wine," Auguste said, taking a sip from his own glass.

The man wasn't so bad, Linus thought, drinking so as to not appear impolite. A little odd, certainly, but he would be, too, if he'd been charged to look after a forgotten cathedral. Come to think of it, he didn't know where the rector lived—he'd never actually seen Auguste enter or leave the building. Maybe Auguste's quarters were here. Linus snorted. Maybe he slept in the crypt. Or standing upright on a beam with his limbs retracted like a bird, still wearing his black suit. But that was ridiculous. He'd probably seen him leave at some point and was just misremembering again.

"Can I get your thoughts on something?" Linus asked on impulse.

Auguste smiled. "Is this perchance about your lady friend?"

"I guess I'm not sure what to do about Savannah. Her vacation time is almost up, and she doubts her supervisor will agree to a transfer, so..."

"...so what are you doing?"

"So what are we doing."

Auguste nodded, his long, beaked nose dunking and dunking into a pool of shadow. "Do you see yourself marrying her one day?"

"I don't... no."

"No? Or you don't know?"

Linus shrugged.

"I know affairs of the heart are complicated, but we mustn't let our own desires take precedence over another person's well-being. If there is no future between the two of you, then it would be selfish for you to make her think there is." Auguste leaned closer. "The fault would lie squarely with you."

Linus could hardly argue with that logic. He'd come close to breaking up with Savannah a few times—not even during fights, just at moments when he'd gazed at her across the room and realized that the distance between them might as well have been polar. Each time, the thought of what his mother would have wanted stopped him from going further. Now he was hearing from someone else— someone whose job it was to provide counsel—confirmation of his doubts. He felt, for lack of a better word, absolved.

In rare moments, Auguste sounded almost fatherly. Yes, the man sometimes got a little pushy, but wasn't that also typical of parents (especially the parents of classical musicians)? And, yes, on a couple of occasions he laid on the guilt, but wasn't that typical of Catholics?

"It looks like the cleaners are about done with reassembly," the rector said, standing. "I will leave you to it."

The next few hours passed slowly: there was the tuning, then some arguing about the agreed-upon cost, and then the settling of the bill. When Linus finally slumped down at the organ that evening, he could no longer muster the motivation to practice. At least he could try out the 64' stop, he thought. Few organists have such a privilege.

He played a short passage from the toccata. As expected, he couldn't even hear the tone. He could, though, feel the vibrations snake up his fingers and arms and into his chest. He chuckled at the weird sensation.

With some sudden, inexplicable trepidation, he combined the 64' and the 42'.

Again, he heard nothing, but this time he could barely even feel the tone. As he sat there with his fingers still on the keys, trying to reason through the science of it all, the cathedral began to shake.

The shaking lasted only a few seconds. Having lived in California as a child, Linus was no stranger to earthquakes, but nevertheless this one made his heart stutter. By the time he'd calmed down, he couldn't think of anything to do but laugh. Maybe the piece was cursed after all!

He could have stayed longer, but, taking the earthquake as a sign that he needed to call it a day, he packed up his stuff and headed for the bus stop, almost slipping when he stepped on something soft and wet in the dark. He lifted his foot—a dead crow with blood worming out of its beak. Sighing, he scraped his shoe against the curb.

"Oh my god, you're bleeding!" was the first thing Savannah said when Linus got home. She rushed up to him, dabbing at the edge of his nose with her sleeve. Seeing his surprise, she added, "You didn't know you were bleeding?"

He rubbed at his nose himself and came away with some rusted copper under his fingernails. "Maybe it was the earthquake," he said.

"Earthquake?"

"Yeah, like half an hour ago."

"Huh, I didn't feel it." She frowned. "But why would an earthquake make your nose bleed?"

"Stress? It's like enough fine. It doesn't look like a lot of blood."

"You blame a lot on stress these days," she said.

Linus went into the bathroom to wash his hands. Savannah followed, leaning against the doorframe as he scrubbed under his nails. He peered at her reflection in the mirror. She was wearing all the rings from when they'd met plus a couple he'd never seen before. One appeared to be made of obsidian—for protection, if he remembered correctly from one of her impromptu lectures on the magical properties of gemstones.

"What's your plan, exactly, once you've mastered the song?" Savannah asked.

"I'm going to play it," he said.

"It's not a church song."

"I'll put on a separate concert."

"And then what?"

"It seems like there's a specific answer you want me to give," he said, barely concealing his irritation. He dried his hands and pushed past her.

"I'm just wondering," she said, "what your end game is. Okay, you put on a concert. Then what? You keep putting on concerts, hoping someone from the Met will contact you? Help me out here."

"I try not to think too far ahead."

She snared his wrist but he shook off her hand. "Come back home with me," she said. "We'll figure out what to do about your career together." Even angry, she still had that natural grace that had drawn him to her. It was the grace of a hostess, he realized, of someone who threw dinner parties, who headed parent-teacher association meetings. His mother wouldn't have wanted Savannah to miss out on all that.

"I think we should break up," he said.

She slammed the bathroom door between them. After a few seconds, the door opened again. She emerged gripping a wad of wet toilet paper.

"Why is this so important to you?" she asked.

"Why is this so important to *you*?"

She stared at him in disbelief. Then she was pulling her pants down over one hip and scrubbing at the flesh there with the toilet paper. The bruise appeared as the makeup disappeared, the size of a large pomegranate and about as red.

"Shit," he said.

"You've never been a calm sleeper," she said, "but now it's like something takes hold of you at night. You're spending so much time playing at that church that you're starting to sound like that priest. 'Like enough'? If I have to, I'll talk to him and convince him to ban you from playing."

Linus felt too consumed by guilt to try to argue her down from the threat. "I'm sorry," he said, pulling her into a hug partly to soothe her but mostly so he could stop staring at the bruise. Whispering reassurances, he managed to wring a promise from her to wait on talking to Auguste, at least until he'd had some time to "process" (what, exactly, he wasn't entirely sure, but she liked that word). That night he insisted on sleeping on the floor.

She was gone when Linus awoke the next morning. He'd been roused by a chill he couldn't quite explain until he noticed the window was wide open. A crow pecked at something on the ledge. "Shoo, shoo," he said, flapping his hands violently, worried the bird would fly into the apartment before he could close the window. The crow eyed him in a way that he could describe only as mocking, and took off.

He checked his phone—no texts or missed calls. No hastily written note tacked up or weighed down, either. All of Savannah's belongings, including her purse, were exactly where she had left them. The only exception was her rings, which were also gone. Well, that made sense. She refused to leave the house without them.

The only logical explanation was that she had gone for a walk, though he struggled to imagine how she might have left without waking him. Linus made himself a cup of coffee and sat down to wait. As he drank, he noticed there was still some blood under his fingernails, probably from that nosebleed yesterday.

When she didn't return after an hour, he texted. And when she didn't respond after another hour, he started to panic, unable to fathom where she might have traveled in this dying city without a car—that was, until he remembered her words from last night.

She might have decided to talk to Auguste anyway. Linus threw on some sweats and hurried to the church.

When he arrived, Auguste was polishing the altar. "Morning, Linus," he said when he heard him approaching, quickly turning around and folding his hands behind his back.

"Morning," Linus said. "Weird question, but have you seen Savannah today by any chance?"

The rector looked confused. "Not since you introduced us," he said. "Should I have seen her?"

"I thought she might have come to talk to you."

"About?"

"It's complicated."

"I see," Auguste said, sinking into one of the pews. His clothes reeked of cleaning solution, as if he'd been scrubbing for hours. "Would I be correct in assuming that the two of you finally had a conversation?"

"Mm."

"It went poorly, then."

"I'm not sure where things stand," Linus admitted. He gazed up at the ceiling, distracted for a second by the shadows writhing there.

"What a shame," Auguste said. "Still, we do what we must to heed the soul's calling. We have no other choice."

He left to do some more cleaning. Linus climbed upstairs and sat down at the console. It was true: he couldn't imagine himself ever doing anything besides this, just this. Savannah would be a wonderful partner to another person. But to him she was a manacle.

Once again, the rector was right. How unfortunate that this church was on the brink of closure. Auguste could be of so much help to so many people.

Absently, Linus returned his attention to the shadows on the ceiling. Souls were always writhing in depictions of hell, he thought. But maybe they were dancing to music only they could hear.

The honking of a car brought him back to himself. Checking his phone, he was shocked to see that more than an hour had passed since he sat down, and that while he was preoccupied, he'd missed a strangely formal text from Savannah. *I have decided to return home early*, the text read. *It is too difficult to see you right now. I will send for my things erelong.*

All of this—it wasn't like her. Trying to put the unease out of his mind, Linus began to practice. When he pulled the Contraposaune stop, something rattled in the pipes, and Savannah's obsidian ring fell out.

There was a deep scratch across the face of the obsidian, as if it had been made by a talon. An unnameable fear overtook him. But just as he was about to dial 911 on his phone (what would he even say to the dispatcher?), a seedling of doubt sprouted in his mind. Had he actually seen that ring on her yesterday? He was like enough just misremembering again. All that stress and disturbed sleep. The sheet music flapped its wings to a breeze from nowhere. Yes, everything was going to be fine.

He resumed his playing. How freely his fingers moved now in spite of the palsy, climbing—no, leaping over one another. For the first time in years, he was in possession of himself again.

The part he never told anyone, the part he'd tried his best to forget, was that he'd seen that truck coming on the way home from the organ lesson. He'd registered it out of the corner of his eye, seconds before the impact, and had tried to say, *Mom, watch out.* He'd tried to reach out with his left hand to grab the wheel. But the words hadn't come out. His body hadn't moved.

Lying there, watching birds circle. The smell of iron heavy and sharp, ambulance sirens shrieking somewhere close but not close enough. He'd touched his left pinky to her right. Or, for all he knew, he'd only dreamed he did.

The midpoint came and went, but Linus didn't feel the least bit tired. He could play like this forever, he realized, first for this congregation and then for the visitors who would come from around the globe to listen, just play and play, powered as if by some mechanism that connected all the way down to the silent song at the bottom of the world.

An excerpt from

YOU PEOPLE

by NIKITA LALWANI

NIA

SHE WAS AT THE crossing with a song in her head, grateful for the warm lick of sun in the sky, waiting for the traffic to pass. The pavement, too, was starting to fill with people, it was almost time for the monthly street market.

The road to the restaurant was blocked off at one end. She couldn't see through to Vesuvio, the view was obstructed by a large white van and a small crowd. They were gathered outside the Polish greasy spoon, stretching back toward the Aussie pub. She could recognize some of them—the guys from the Chinese place, the attendants from the launderette. A man and a woman in blue Tesco polo shirts were conferring across the narrow part of the road, near the betting shop.

They were staring at something or someone. She followed the eyeline and saw him: a man in a black uniform, only then registering the small, luminous yellow rectangles stitched on the front, the walkie-talkie in his hand, the words UK BORDER AGENCY on his back. A red-haired woman walked out and stood behind him, bronze highlights crowning her short figure, clothed in the same outfit, speaking into her radio and attaching it to her chest.

Oh, shit, Nia thought. Elene. Is she legal? She must be. Surely.

The crowd was pushing in a little now and she couldn't see the Tesco duo anymore. There were about ten people in Nia's way, give or take a few, mostly men of varying sizes, rumbling with a low, apprehensive energy. They emanated heat, there was a smell that was a jumble of all their different years.

"Where you *going?*" one of them shouted, emphasizing the final word, as though kicking off a football chant or a protest march. "Where you *going?*"

"*Leave him!*" said another.

She waited, tentatively pushing herself up onto her toes, on the outskirts. She wanted to call out, let Elene know she was there, but her voice would have no chance against the noise, the volume was increasing with every minute. God knows who they were taking away. "Him" suggested it was one of the cooks. Or even the proprietor himself—was it possible?

Her phone was going against her hand in the front pocket of her jacket. She had long ago switched off the ringtone, so that it was only capable of a faint vibration, because there was really only one person who called her these days. She pulled it out with jittery fingers, worried that someone was ringing from Vesuvio. She hadn't even considered the possibility that this chaos might have reached her own place of work.

But it was her sister. She pressed the button required to reject the call.

The last time she had answered a call from Mira, there was honestly no rhyme or reason to it, in fact, it was a kind of idleness that meant Nia pressed ACCEPT. And then, before clocking what she'd done, she had to speak to her.

"Banana brains!" Nia said into the receiver, before she could get her guard up. She was upstairs at the restaurant, sorting out the mini fridge behind the bar.

"It's not funny, Nia," came the reply, plaintive in spite of itself.

"Tomato head!" Nia said, as if all the old nicknames could form a carpet between them, a magic corridor of embroidered fabric from here to Newport, shrink time and space, put them in the same protected continuum.

"Nia, stop it."

"Peach face! How's it going?"

"Nia, it's two weeks I've been trying you for—"

"What is it?" The words cut through quickly, suddenly sharp. "What does she want, then?"

"She's bad, Nia—you don't know how she's been, it's worse than usual—"

She could hear a scuffle of voices in the background, the strident tones of their mother. She couldn't decipher her words, but the energy was intense.

"How much does she want?" Nia said.

"Nia, for fuck's sake, what do you want to always be bringing it down to that for, it's not just cash—"

"How much?"

Mira didn't reply. Instead, Nia could hear her mother's voice making its way loudly through the noise until it was right up close to the phone.

"Who you talking to? Who you talking to? You talking to that stuck-up bitch in London? Tell that fucking ungrateful slut something from me—"

It went muffled then, Mira had covered the phone with her hand. When she came back, she sounded worried.

"Nia?" So tentative and vulnerable that it made Nia screw up her eyes.

"How much?" she said.

"Nia, don't be like that."

"How much, Mira?"

"I've been doing the skips again—"

"What the fuck, Mira."

"Nia, she just wants to see you—"

She hung up. It was her sweet baby sister, Mira, yes, but she dropped it on the bar counter, the phone, after ending the call. It was suddenly burning, or so it felt, and she put herself downstairs, into another room, got away from its radioactive waves. *She just wants to see you. Just.*

Still, after an hour, she went back, held the pernicious thing in her hand, and rang the bank. She put fifty quid in Mira's account. It was a significant part of her week's wages. By "doing the skips," Mira meant she was doing what they had done whenever things got to their worst and their mother was out of action—gone to the dumpsters of the local supermarkets after dark and rifled through the packages for unused food. The safest parts were from the bakery— bread rolls, Danish pastries, bagels, all baked that morning and thrown away that night. They didn't ever take the fish or meat, even if they were in three layers of plastic wrap, not just because you might get sick, but because by that point, if you were rifling through trash, you weren't about to start cooking when you got back.

She was fifteen now. Nia thought of her small face—you could always read it as easily as those Love Heart sweets with the messages printed on them—imagined those peachy cheeks full of almond crois- sant, and retched suddenly, holding her hand tightly over her stomach.

After half an hour, she found a way to leave her shift early. It was unlike her to cry sickness at work like this, but she couldn't shake the nausea. The air was sticky and dingy when she emerged from Vesuvio, there was very little light on the street, and Nia was muffled by the absence, as though it were oxygen that was missing rather than illumi- nation. Something was wrong with the streetlamp. She stepped around a heap of glass on the curb. Twinkling and sharp, the diamanté mass of crystals on the road was lying next to a car with a crater smashed into its window. She walked quickly to the Underground station, speeding up on seeing Sue, the regular sleeper on that patch. She was visible from a distance, arranging her dull navy sleeping bag and provisions near the Tube entrance. Nia tried to get past without fishing through her bag for the coins she'd normally pass to her on the way home.

"Oh dear," Sue said when their eyes invariably locked. She had a stripy woolen hat on and her ears were poking out of her long brown hair. She frowned and pushed her glasses up the bridge of her nose, her pale digits in fingerless gloves. "Is it a difficult day today, love? No good?" She had been sleeping on that bit of the street since before Nia arrived and she had a routine for this particular hour before midnight—she'd often be arranging or replacing the big piece of cardboard underneath her bedding, at other times she'd be sitting cross-legged and smoking, acknowledging passersby, occasionally chatting with some of them. If it was very late, she might have a can or two sitting near her rucksack.

Nia nodded, tears welling, feeling regret once she was in through the ticket barriers.

"Sue, I'm sorry...," she muttered, although it was to herself.

She had a scarf and another pair of gloves for Sue in her bag, as it happened—had picked them up in a charity shop for a pittance. She usually gave her something like that once a week, she'd accept more than she'd reject, Sue, and they were relatively friendly. Probably she made Nia think of her mom in some way, she didn't overthink it, but she looked forward to seeing her. She knew her preferences by now, to get Sue a fruit salad rather than a doughnut if she was feeling flush when she went into Tesco, for example.

But that day she had spoken to her little sister; it was all laced up so tightly, Nia's heart, and she didn't want to look at her. She felt so lonely, and she knew Sue had it worse, but Nia didn't have any space in her chest for it—all in all, the whole thing was what her mother would have called a shit sandwich.

SHAN

Thalai muzhuguthal. Literal translation: to pour water over someone's head. Actual meaning: to cut off a relationship. Shan is soothing his confusion as he walks, soothing it through the repetition of this phrase, polishing it over like a piece of brass. He is thinking of

Devaki and the many unsuccessful attempts he has made to get ahold of her. He wants, of course, to believe that her silence is due to anger, rather than because she is dead. But if she were pouring water on their marriage, surely she wouldn't do it this way?

Ava is always talking about finger strength when it comes to climbing—training your capacity to hold on to crucial crags of rock as you ascend. That is how it feels when he rifles through his past with Devaki—he is trying his best to grasp onto clues that will help him believe that she is alive.

It is true that as a couple, he and Devaki had specialized in awful arguments. He would leave the soiled furnace of their words when it was too overwhelming—and walk around outside for hours—coming back to find that she was a wreck, shaking with the spent violence of a thousand tears. He was careful with her then, not always hiding his shameful pleasure at this: that she cared so much about the two of them, had cried so much. That she loved him the way he did her, with a rueful obsession, each of them destined to make the other bend in their direction.

She was the academic, the one with a permanent lab position. He was the one who couldn't get a steady job at the university. And, of course, there was Karu: the impulsive dreaming up of their child's future was what united them most poetically but also what divided them. She ran the house. She was so competent, so unequivocally beautiful, so kind when she felt it was right... just so exactly Devaki. Her only public flaw, as she saw it, was her weight—she wrestled with her appetite, which fluctuated cruelly and held her hostage in its sudden emotional manifestations. Privately, there was her wildness: part of her allure, but injurious too. It inflamed every spat with acute urgency, as though they were about to go out to a firing squad if they didn't get to the truth.

There was that saying—do you want to be happy in marriage or do you want to be right? He had come across it in one of those books sold on the footpath in Jaffna, amid a raft of paperbacks that all seemed to be versions of *How to Win Friends and Influence People*.

Now he wants nothing more than for them to be stuck in the worst fight of their lives, a shocking, seismic disagreement of international proportions. How wonderful it would be if this loss of dialogue between them was just because she was full of silent fury. Radiantly alive, and full of fury. He would be happy with that.

He is inside and outside the world at once. Sometimes when he bathes in the morning, he is so spent by this simple act that he sits on the plastic flooring in the towel after he has dried himself, unable to get up and dress. He keeps his eyes open, craving the fevered, salty melt that would surely come with tears. But there is nothing there. He just shivers instead. If he closes his eyes, he sees blood, and then comes the image of his son. If he is not careful, he will hear his son speak.

Crush and fade, slip and follow. He is making a concerted effort to walk away from the restaurant in a calm way and to avoid thinking about the immigration van that he can see out of the corner of his eye as he leaves Vesuvio behind him. Very soon he is surrounded by people, due to a temporary market on one of the short roads between the restaurant and bus stop. Cheese, potted jams, breads, and pickles—each stand is oddly specific with regard to contents, and customers are hovering over these goods as though they are precious stones.

There is a man behind Shan who shares his frustration at getting through the crowd, he is a Japanese man of similar build who is more resolute than he is when it comes to keeping up speed. He moves along the street with an open book in one hand, the leash of his dog in the other, stubbornly continuing to read as he pushes his way through the mass. Stops his reading only to cross the road, and then resumes the curious, fervent task of consuming his book while walking. The golden-haired dog at his side accommodates its owner without complaint, bends in its body to stay on the pavement. Shan watches them disappear around the corner, admiring the man's resolve. There is a lot to be said for such persistence.

Barely ten minutes go by before he receives Ava's text.

Come back. They are gone. Elene say they drive away.

And there you are. It is oddly deflating to read it. There is even still time to make it back before his shift begins. He must go back, but he can't feel relieved. What is there to stop them from returning?

He is back on their street within minutes of receiving the text, and the van is indeed gone, leaving an open space of some relief when he looks down the clear road. But when he walks under the striped plastic awning at the front of Vesuvio, in through the front door, the shaking begins again. It's still too early for the other cooks or Tuli, and so he tries his best to begin as normal, opens his hat and apron so that they are ready to wear. Ava sees him, clocks the disturbance in him. He has been staring at the items for too long, leaning against a chair at one point.

"Is a shock," she says quietly, moving in to help him to sit down. "You need to stop for a minute, Shan. Just wait."

He shakes her off and is up again, walking back out through the kitchen into the yard, the same route exactly, over the same back wall, blindly, frowning hard, walking, just walking till he reaches a thick green hedge of some sort to his left side. People can see you, but they don't see what you are. He still wants more than anything to shout, the need is fermenting dangerously inside him. It is a basic right, surely, to be able to shout without fear of condemnation? He stops and puts his face in the wet needles, immerses in the sensation of a hundred tiny sharp points against his skin, and only then does he feel the demons begin to leave his body.

Later, he is working hard when he hears Tuli breeze into the main space of the restaurant with his usual greetings. Ava's voice joins the noise, she is relaying everything with pattering speed. For a moment Shan thinks about going to join in with the explanations. The boss would probably receive him the way he does everyone: with a show of warmth and understanding, even though news of a raid on the street will be unwelcome and bring its own tensions. But he can't trust himself to talk. There is no benefit to seeking out an audience with Tuli right now, he thinks. Ava will do the needful. Let Ava do it.

—You People *by Nikita Lalwani is out this spring from McSweeney's.*

I DRINK A GLASS OF WATER

FOUR POSTHUMOUS STORIES BY STEPHEN DIXON

Introduction by POROCHISTA KHAKPOUR

Portrait on following page by
HANNA SOMETHING

INTRODUCTION

by POROCHISTA KHAKPOUR

LIFE VERSUS ART. THIS was the concept that hovered around our heads, us young aspiring writers in the then second-best writing program in the country (Johns Hopkins Writing Seminars). The question was fashionable at the time. You could be the writer who had discipline and craft and skills, or you could be the writer who *really* lived, whose adventures were the anecdotes that made up intricate plots, whose characters were based on a cast so real they were called "larger-than-life." Our program was split between those camps, and the question—if it was a question, even—was never resolved. I recall regularly staying out all night with my set of loud, messy, rebellious types, while other students were back in their apartments by dinnertime. We found this amusing but easy to understand: They were in the camp that chose art; we had chosen life. Different roads, that was all.

"Where the hell would you get an idea like that? Dichotomies? When, ever? I mean, really, you are asking where do *I* stand?" my most beloved professor and mentor, Stephen Dixon, asked me in his office one day when I brought up this idea of the two camps, thinking I was really onto something. But his face quickly let me know that was not the case.

"You're kidding, right?" he went on.

"Yes," I lied sweetly with a tight smile.

"Good," he grumbled. It always felt like there was an invisible cigarette he was taking a long drag off of between his fingers. Dixon was constantly teetering into exasperation but never so much that it felt like resentment, thank goodness.

The last time I saw Stephen Dixon was seventeen years ago, back when I was a student, and I don't even remember the exact moment. I had no idea he was going to retire just four years after I left. I think I imagined him existing forever in exactly that form, as our forever mentor, sighing and groaning and rolling his eyes, somehow always still lovingly. Did we have a proper goodbye, even? The night before our graduation, a group of the worst troublemakers in our cohort and I, plus my visiting hometown best friend, all piled into someone's run-down station wagon and drove to Atlantic City after hours of drinking at a pub in the heart of Baltimore. I think we made it there around 4:00 a.m., and all I remember is how awful the dawn light felt, how we drank even more, how someone threw up outside the station wagon window, how I made out with a friend while squished in the middle seat on the way home, and how we got back in time for short, ugly naps just before the graduation ceremony. Did he see me then? Or was our most memorable meeting the last, weeks before graduation, when I went to his office just after unsuccessfully attempting suicide among the tulips of Guilford Park, when the pressures of my thesis were becoming too much, especially when paired with addiction and mental illness? In that meeting he tore an orange in two parts with his bare hands and handed me half, and I ate it along with him right into that jagged wet wild, a face full of orange juice and pulp and tears, as I asked him what road to take in life. He was not put off by the question and didn't hesitate to answer it: he thought I was a novelist, not a short story writer; that I should go back to New York and not teach but do real stuff, like drive a cab or tend bar. Like he had. Eventually I should publish books (in the end he published thirty-five books and over seven hundred stories, which he felt any of us could do with some discipline), get married, have kids—all like he had. Life. Art.

It sounded okay. In the end, I did teach and I did not get married or have kids. But I published. And maybe he knew it, maybe he did not. I can't remember seeing him in the audience when I returned to campus in 2008 to give a reading to the Writing Seminars after my first novel's debut. The second time I was back on campus to read was in November 2019, just under twenty-four hours after his death.

There are few humans I loved more than Stephen Dixon. Not only was he the model of a writer for me, but he was also the model of a human.

Art, life. Not only did we learn so much as his students, but we learned as his readers. And that's something everyone should be glad to hear, because he left a tremendous body of work. Anyone can access him in this way, which he would argue was his most genuine form of connection—he *was* his writing, more than any writer I have ever encountered.

He wrote daily, often a story a day. How? He didn't have to choose a camp. Life *was* art, and he included it all, unfiltered—the line between fiction and nonfiction was irrelevant. We knew all about his wife and daughters, his home office, his bed and bathroom, his garage and car, the women he slept with in his twenties, the run-ins big and small that made him who he was. It's rare to read the writing of a man that gets *this* personal, but that was the reality with Steve. He would line-edit your stories so much that you assumed syntax and diction were his only concerns, but then in conference he'd have you bawling into the guts of an orange, confessing suicidal ideation, only to match your stories of adversity with his own.

You always knew you were okay, because he was around. And I guess that's maybe why I never got back in touch. I thought he'd always be around. Besides, he let us know how much he hated email. He was always brutally honest, and that honesty was a bit terrifying. He made it clear that teaching, giving readings, being interviewed, going to the grocery store, parking his car, answering the phone—all of it was a nuisance, as it interrupted his one purpose: to have writing time. Only time with his wife and daughters took priority over writing.

I still feel intimidated just reading his stories again, sensing his irritation with a reader who can't keep up with his spiraling logic in the twists and tangles of his neuroses, not unlike his constant infuriation at agents and editors and at the endless politics of mainstream publishing. Steve never had time for things like that, though he made all the time in the world for others.

He loved underdogs, for example, and ultimately I think that is how he learned to love himself. I was an underdog, too, and he saw that in me. He was the only reason I survived that year. And his sheet of carefully composed, typewritten line-edits of my story "Spectacle," which I wrote in my final weeks in his workshop, was what led me to write my first novel, *Sons and Other Flammable Objects*—which kept basically the same story line but converted into what he thought was its rightful form. Steve had seen me get brutalized one too many times in class workshops—I was one of the only non–Ivy League students, one of the youngest too—and he always found a way to rescue my stories from the class's default of pure assault. I'll never quite know if it was because of that protectiveness or because the story was actually good that he encouraged "Spectacle."

Does it really matter? I can imagine him asking.

No, I can imagine myself lying.

I was invited to speak at his memorial, where I met his daughters, both as smart and lovely and interesting as I had imagined. It was on February 27, 2020, in the final weeks of normalcy before most of the country would be in pandemic lockdown. The Murmrr Ballroom, in Brooklyn, was packed with oddballs, and it had a funny psychedelic sheen to its lighting. In all my photos of the audience, every white-haired person appears like a blue-haired Dr. Seuss character. We laughed more than I thought we would laugh that night. The stories everyone told were uproarious and irreverent—you felt that his life, just like his art, involved a very lively cast.

A few weeks later, I spoke on the phone for hours with an author who is writing his biography, and I laughed and cried through so many memories. Just weeks later, I received a package in the mail: a half dozen hardcover editions of books Dixon authored, from his personal library. The biographer was assisting the family in cleaning out his office. I held the books tight; traced their jackets for dust; even, like a character in a bad melodrama, sniffed the pages in case they could take me back to him for a moment—and then I placed them in the order they had come in and piled them by my desk. The books have become an altar of sorts: a totem I face every single day, every single writing day.

He would have noticed that to me "a day" now equals "a writing day," and maybe that would have made him prouder than anything. That was all him, after all.

When I received the stories that appear in this issue, I was touched to see that they were scans of typewritten pages in PDF form, a few with typos, even, which felt triumphant to spot (line-editing the line-edit king!), precious in their raw humanness. The stories, unsurprisingly, were stunning. The subjects also felt so familiar, so in keeping with the concerns of the Dixon canon: writer finishing a story, man meeting a future wife, New York City flashbacks, Maryland suburbia, the burdens and joys of being the father of daughters, a wife's passing, aging, small talk and the negotiations of everyday life, the body's failures (pills, catheters, hospitals, hospice), everyday urban sustenance (sandwiches, coffee, wine, fried oysters, smoked salmon, fish burgers). And there were the classic Dixonian themes: shame, tenderness, anxiety, intimacy, frustration, love, loss. And there was that trademark Dixon sound: long, winding sentences that operate like arteries for every anxiety imaginable, together creating a pulsing network of honest internal monologues. It felt so good to turn those pages and to be so deep in his head and to find that place a familiar one, to know that at the end of his life he was still at one with his art.

And then the pages stopped. It happened in that premature dark of November 2019, in my office in Queens, with just the sounds of the city—subways, cabs, birds, the hum and rattle of pipes—filling in where he left off. I wanted so badly for there be more (and somehow I suspect there must be, that there has to be more to come). But the way his words, his precise and passionate art, bled from the page right into the exterior landscape of my life, so many realities removed, reminded me: When you really live, and when you really tackle that life in your art, the pages never quite end. The narration might drop out, but the story is still in motion.

If done right, the border blurs, the boundaries of life and of art fade into each other—your breath exists alongside your characters'; the sounds of your city overlay the sounds of the protagonist's city; the distractions nagging at the corners of your consciousness are suddenly incorporated into the psyche of an ingenue cliffhanging. There is no real finale, since the world continues long after we're gone. Dixon's storytelling was like a house that's larger on the inside than on the outside. When I finished these stories, I was left with a similar sense: that we are all just players in a story he wrote long ago, which has a life now past his own. And just like in his book *Interstate*, when the father dies in the final pages of the first section and the story continues without the father's close third point of view, here we are, left with the roles he has written for us.

It makes sense that in this batch of stories, one is called "Finding an Ending" and begins: "I can't seem to finish the story I've been writing." If that isn't an author who knows death is on the way, I don't know what is. Another, "The Lost One," begins: "Good morning, my dearie. Sleep well?" And the answer is "I want to go home." And to double down on the Dixonian flourishes, he pushes it deeper: "You don't understand. Or you're not listening. I want to go home because I want to die there." By the time we get to "Oh My Darling"—I won't spoil the central dilemma there—we know Dixon's fixation is on the idea of decline. He's not dealing with decline generally, but his own degeneration after a long, colorful life, and only with the recognition that the world around him will continue its spins of colorful lives when he's gone. In these stories there is nothing nostalgic, sentimental, or fever-pitched—the emotional frequencies he sometimes favored—and the obsessive register is there still, but it's muted and almost revels in the mundane. Life, as cliché as it is to say, does indeed go on, these pages seem to say—and so does art, no matter who comes and goes. The stories get told no matter which storytellers enter or exit.

The altar of his books faces me each day, daring me to create something lasting like that. I don't know if I will, but at least I know I was taught how to.

OUT FOR A SPIN

by STEPHEN DIXON

WE'RE IN A CAR, she's at the wheel, I don't know where we're going.

"If I may ask, where we going?"

The car's a convertible, the top's down. She doesn't hear me. She puts her hand behind her ear and says "What's that you said?"

"Where we going? And why are you driving so fast? And must we have the top down?"

"It's a convertible. That's what the top's for. To come down in nice weather."

"So you can hear me now?"

"I can hear you. But what were you saying before when I couldn't hear you?"

"'Where we going?'"

"What?"

"You must be kidding me now."

"What?"

"You can hear me."

"Shout it. I can't hear you."

I shout: "You can hear me."

"Yes, now I can. But I asked what were you saying before when I couldn't hear you?"

"'Where we going?'"

"To school."

"What do you mean?"

"Now I was only kidding. We're long past school. Teaching and studenting. Driving our kids to school. Picking them up after school and driving them home to whatever after-school activity they were doing. Dance. Swimming. Voice lessons. Long past. We're retired, no longer part of the work and parenting force. Our kids have long been all grown up and one of them is looking after kids of her own."

"So where we going?"

"I'm sorry. Lost you again. You have to speak louder if you want me to hear you. If you don't want me to hear you, speak as low as you've been doing."

"Let's stop the car and put the top down. I mean up. Then I could hear you better and you to me. I'm also afraid of the sun. My dermatologist told me to stay out of it. Or when I have to be in it, to wear a cap of some kind, though one that completely covers my head, even when the sun isn't out and the day is cloudy. The pre-cancerous scalp lesions I'm prone to. And is cloud spelled with a *u* or *w*? I was just wondering. Funny how the mind wanders."

"With a *u*, I think. Or now that I think of it, maybe it's a *w*. For sure, either. But you don't need to stop and park to put the top up or down. This car can do it while you're driving, and in a matter of seconds. Here. Watch." She presses a button on the dashboard and the top comes up and snaps into place. Then she presses the button next to the button she just pressed and the top goes down and snaps into place.

"No, keep it up. My scalp. The sun."

She presses the first button she pressed and the top goes up and snaps into place. "See how easy it is. A child could do it. And it took no more than five seconds, so no danger to the driver's visibility of the road. But of course—"

"'You wouldn't want a child driving the car'; I know. So again, where you taking us? And where'd you get this car?"

"You know perfectly well."

"Let's say I don't. It's new and it must go for forty to fifty thousand, and with that up-and-down convertible top mechanism, maybe more. You own it or renting it or just borrowing it? You going out with a very rich guy and he bought you it?"

"Sure, that's it. How'd you find out?"

"Anybody I know? For whom do you know who has such an expensive car or is so generous to buy you one?"

"What *q* do you want me to answer first?"

"*Q* for *question*, you're asking?"

"What else could it be for?"

"*Q* for *quick* and *q* for *quibble* and *q* for *quixotic* and *Quonset hut* and *guacamole* and—"

"I believe the last *q* should be a *g*, and what's any of those got to do with what we were talking about?"

"Nothing, or maybe something to all those questions. But I was just saying the first words that start with *q* that came into my head or out of my mouth. *Quibble*."

"You did that one."

"That's right. My short-term memory is getting shorter. I think that's right. Soon it'll be so short it'll… what? Fill in the word for me, will ya, hon? I can't come up with one, and I'm trying. I'm really trying."

"I can't come up with one right now either. Or I'm just not interested enough in what you're saying to continue this train of talk."

"So again—and I know I'm repeating myself, I think more to continue the conversation than for any other reason—where'd you get this car and where you driving us to?"

"As I said, so I'm also repeating myself, you know perfectly well where I got it and the reason behind my having it. I had an accident. It was the other driver's fault, of course, so don't blame me. Fortunately, neither of us was hurt. I needed a replacement car while mine was being repaired. I wanted a loaner, a term new to me, but the body shop said I'd have to get a rental. Look at me. First time I heard the word *loaner* when it's applied to a car and I'm already using it as if it were part of my everyday vocabulary. The auto-rental place didn't have on its lot any car smaller and less elaborately equipped than this one, so they gave me it for the rate of a much smaller and simpler car and one that doesn't use up so much gas. I've come to like it, despite its drawbacks, ecological and aesthetic—do you?"

"It's a bit big and too showy for my tastes, and I'm really against a gas guzzler and also a convertible for the reason I gave before. Sun. Scalp. And yes, I guess I did know where you got it, but the question of where you're taking us I don't. But maybe you'd like me to take over the wheel and then you could ask me where I'm driving us to, which is what we used to do when we went on long trips years ago— sharing the driving. To Maine, for instance, early on before we had kids. First time we didn't make the drive in one day was when you were six months pregnant with our first child and we had to break up the trip. I'm glad we did because I got to like Kennebunkport for a night and so did, eventually, you and the kids. Running on the beach. 'Try and catch Daddy.' Dining at the Breakwaters Inn and sleeping and breakfasting at the Green Heron across the street. That was fun. We don't have fun like that anymore, it seems. And once we drove in two days to Durham, though I forget what for. Either you were giving a lecture or I was giving a reading. Or maybe it was Raleigh, or that third city in the so-called Research Triangle, and through the Great Smoky Mountains. I think I said a number of times during the drive till I tired you out with the remarks, and if the kids were with us, then the kids: 'Where's the smoke? I don't see any smoke. And these mountains aren't that great, in size or to look at. They might not even be mountains, they're so small; maybe just hills. How many feet does a hill have to be to be called a mountain?'"

"You couldn't have said that. It was the Blue Ridge Mountains we took to get to Chapel Hill."

"Then I probably said, if I know me, something like 'There's nothing blue about these mountains. Neither the mountains themselves nor the sky above them.'"

"Maybe you did. It would be like you, and to repeat it, or something like it, long after you should have stopped. But I also forget if the trip took us one or two days. If it was two, then we stopped off somewhere for the night, though where that was I also forget. And those aren't examples of sympathetic forgetfulness, if there is such a thing, and if there isn't, maybe there should be. Good idea, though, your taking over the wheel. I've been driving for too long already and my eyes are tired."

"You've only been driving for twenty minutes at the most. Your eyes couldn't be tired from driving. It must be from something else."

She stares at me, smiles conspiratorially, I'll call it, then looks back to the road.

"Wise move. Don't get distracted. Keep your eyes peeled to the road and your mind on the driving."

"Tell me, and I know this is clear out of the blue, but why do they call this road a parkway? There's no park or woods or just plain land of any sort around it since we got on it. Just buildings large and small and malls, shopping centers, streets, avenues, gas stations and the like. Hardly a tree. And when a tree, more like a shrub. You needn't answer my question if you don't know the answer. That'll be all right."

"You're going to be surprised by my answer. I haven't a clue why it's called a parkway. It's possible there was once parkland on both sides of it and the city grew around it till all the parkland was choked off. I bet there were once deer and foxes and maybe even bears on both sides of the parkway. Certainly, squirrels. But you tell me. I still don't know where you're going. Just out for a drive to show me the attributes of your expensive rental car and then you'll drive us home and we'll do whatever we typically do inside and outside our home and read a little, newspaper and books, and listen to the five o'clock news on the radio and decide what we want for dinner and then prepare it and cook it if some of it has to be cooked or go out for dinner and then come home and maybe have another drink and then prepare for bed and go to bed but wash up first and get in bed and read a little and then one of us will put his or her book on his or her night table and shut his or her light and soon the other will do the same and we'll kiss goodnight and maybe the kiss will turn into another kiss and then more kisses and we'll take off our bedclothes or for me nothing because I usually come to bed without anything on, and feel each other up and down and you'll get on top or I will or we'll make love another way and after it kiss for the last time tonight and turn over and face the side of the bed each of us is on and say goodnight and maybe only then kiss for the last time tonight and fall asleep pretty fast since neither of us seems to have much trouble getting to sleep and probably dream one or two dreams we'll both forget soon after we wake up and I'll get up two or three times to pee during the night and you might get up once to pee but probably not because you don't have the same problem I have and then sleep some more and both of us will get up around the same time tomorrow morning and wash up and dress and have breakfast or maybe make love before we get out of bed as we seem to do about once every two or three weeks in the morning and one of us will get the newspaper by the mailbox and we'll read different sections of the paper while we're having breakfast and maybe discuss something one of us read in the paper and then we'll wash the dishes, or one of us will, and you'll go into your study and I'll go to our bedroom to work for a couple of hours or more and then we'll have lunch, or you will because I rarely have lunch at home other than for a carrot and celery stalk or two and coffee and a cup of miso soup I'll make, and maybe go to the Y together, before but more likely after lunch to work out and you'll also swim, and sit for about twenty minutes in the sauna there and then take a shower at the Y, or just I will, you prefer to shower at home, and go home or before we go home do a little shop at our neighborhood market or the other market we like to go to especially for its prepared foods, a couple of miles further away from the house, and do all this going from one place to another in this car or mine. And you don't happen to own this car, do you? You didn't impulsively buy it without telling me or consulting with me first?"

"What are you saying? Just talking again to keep the conversation going, because you know I didn't. It's a rental. What else could it be? A loaner, I suppose, but you know that isn't the case with this one. Our auto insurance covers almost half of it for the two weeks the car will be in the body shop. A car smashed into mine. It was completely the other driver's fault. The driver admitted so at the scene of the accident and the police officer summoned to the scene confirmed it. The accident took out my front bumper and right side mirror and right headlight and passenger door and also cracked the windshield. I was lucky I wasn't hurt. Not even a scratch."

"I didn't forget. I've no idea why I gave the impression I did. Even if it had been your fault I wouldn't have criticized you for it. We all get into auto accidents if we drive long enough. I've probably had five or six of them in my driving life and I'd say half of them were my fault. But one question. And of course I'm glad you weren't hurt. I'm still curious where you're taking us now. Just driving to drive and, if I hadn't asked you not to, with the top down, which we never have a chance to do with our two cars, because it's such a nice day?"

"That's it. Nothing more than that. But one question from me to you. When I said 'bumper' before, should I more accurately have said 'fender'? I've never been sure which one it is for the front of the car and which for the back. It was explained to me once by an auto mechanic, or 'technician,' as they like to call them today. Or maybe it was the service person at the front desk who was taking care of me when I brought the car in to get it serviced. But that was long ago, maybe when we still only had one car, and I forget what that person said. So I did know for a while, if I didn't forget by the time the car was ready—I waited for it I remember—and I got the keys back and left the place. To tell you the truth, I feel a little stupid asking you it. And how I found the courage to ask this auto expert, I don't know. It seems like something every driver knows."

"If this will make you happy, I think either will do, though 'bumper' for the front might be better. You can't bump from the back, can you?—though maybe you can. I'd have to think about that. Anyway, don't feel stupid asking the question. I'm not entirely sure myself which is for which, or if one could be for both, so I think I've used them interchangeably. Is that an honest enough answer for you? But back to my original question. And by that I mean the one that comes before any of the others I might have asked and which I seem to have been asking since we started out on this trip—are you just driving because it's such a nice day? Taking us for a little spin, as people used to say?"

"It is a very nice day. Not too warm, not at all cold; no threat of rain. And I would, as you said, prefer to drive with the top down, as it's quite possible, what with the unpredictable weather we've been having, I might not have another day like this while I have this car. And I feel good, and you appear to be in a good mood too, which makes the day even more pleasant. It's always nicer—the day and just being—when we're both in good moods, or in a good mood. Which is it? Which is right, I'm saying?"

"Both seem good. 'In a good mood' might seem better. You still haven't answered my question, though, about where you're taking us, but that's okay. Look, what do you say we just go to lunch? Restaurant of your choosing. The perfect end to the middle of the day."

"I like that. You're usually not that poetic at phrasing things, but you did well there with that 'end to the middle of the day.' I also like your suggestion of lunch. If you're being sincere about leaving it wholly up to me, I know of a good place, and it's not too far from here."

"Fine by me. Let's do it."

She turns the car around and from the directions she's going I know it's a restaurant we've been to a couple of times and liked. Simple. Informal. Not expensive. Good-sized servings. I remember we boxed about half of what we ordered, and we didn't overorder, either, and took it home and had it for lunch the next day. Or she had most of it for lunch the next day. I only had some of the salad, which I now also remember was by that time almost too wilted and oily to eat. A place I can wear sweatpants and a T-shirt to without feeling I'm not appropriately dressed. Delicious, unusual soups. Imaginative sandwiches and salads. Everything "organic," although I'm not absolutely sure what that designation means. And great coffee. Zeke's. Best in Baltimore, supposedly. Choice of dark or light roast. The first time we went there I ordered the dark roast because I thought it was the stronger of the two. But the server told me, when I asked if there really was much difference between the two roasts, that the light, "strange as this might seem, is the stronger one." I still don't understand the reasoning behind that. I did say "How can 'light' be stronger than 'dark,' and I'm talking about coffee?" and she explained, but I guess it didn't sink in or I wasn't listening carefully.

"Good choice," I say as she pulls into a parking space near the restaurant's entrance. "The restaurant, I mean."

"I knew that."

We get out of the car and she takes my hand as we walk to the restaurant. She stops before we get there and, still holding my hand, but tighter now, looks up. "You were right about the sun. Maybe I didn't tell you that. We shouldn't, except at night, and at night it'd spook me to do it, be driving with the top down. You with your precancerous scalp lesions and biannual scalp freezing, as you call it, the dermatologist gives you, and me with the possibility of getting them, since my skin's so much fairer than yours. Though probably less of a chance than you of getting them on my scalp, or maybe no chance, because I have so much more hair on my head than you."

"You think that stops it? The sun can't get through a thick head of hair? Anyway, don't remind me. I mean, that I've gone almost completely bald since we first met. I was lucky it took that long."

"You still pass. But are you sensitive about it? You've never said, and I've never asked."

"Not really. About being sensitive about it. Or just a little to a little more than a little. So, sometimes. But I bet if I was as bald then, or even half as bald, as I am now, you wouldn't have gone for me or been interested in me, or whatever the wording is, or it just would have taken much longer till you didn't think about my baldness anymore, or nowhere near as much as you would have from the start."

"At the start of our relationship? Not true. Entirely untrue. Or at least I don't think so. You had plenty of other fine qualities then that would have made up for it, if you were as short of hair, should we call it?—as you are now."

"But it would have made a little difference."

"Okay, a little. But even that wouldn't have lasted."

"You're sweet."

"It's not that. But all right. Let's go inside. The sun. And I think from now on when I go out—at least when it's sunny, and thick head of hair or not—I ought to always wear a cap or kerchief of some kind too."

We go inside the restaurant. She gives my hand one last squeeze and lets go of it when we get past the door. While we're waiting for a table, we look at the menu on a stand by the entrance.

"Oh, look," she says. "They have my favorite. Fried oysters. I was hoping they would. My lucky day. I've been here for lunch with Barbara a few times the past year and they never seem to have it. But with you, this must be the third time."

"So you're going to have that?"

"What do you think?"

"That you're going to have it. I'm going to stick with what I had the last two times I was here with you. The served-all-day breakfast sandwich. With bacon, not sausages, and the bacon, if they can do it, extra crisp. Comes with grits, which I love."

"Creature of habit. No, so am I. I have my likes and dislikes and my not-so-likes too. But fried oysters, especially the way they're done here, are at the top of my list. This is fun. We should go out for lunch more."

"You won't hear me complain. And we'll share, right? Today I mean. Lunch. You'll let me have one or two of your oysters and in return you can have half my sandwich and however much of the grits you want. That's a good deal, isn't it? Two, maybe just one oyster for half a sandwich and as much of the grits as you want."

"I thought you liked grits."

"I do, I do."

"Anyway, they don't give you that many oysters and I'm not interested in your sandwich or grits, so I'll give you just one oyster. That okay? It depends how many I get."

"Sure, one's enough. You rave about them so much, I just want to taste it."

"Then order the fried oysters instead of the breakfast sandwich."

"No, the breakfast sandwich I know I like."

"Then why are you so willing to give me half of it? Maybe because you know I don't much care for egg sandwiches, particularly scrambled or fried egg sandwiches, even if it has bacon in it, which you know I like. But I will give you one, even if I think there's something a bit shady, or *tricky* might be a better, or kinder, word for it, in your so-called good deal."

"No, not at all. Not in the least. Trust me. I swear. And great. I'm going to finally have a fried oyster. You once offered me one here and I didn't take you up on it because I never liked raw oysters—just the thought of swallowing them whole, which you're supposed to do—so I didn't think I'd like one fried. I don't know what changed my mind, but now the thought of eating a fried oyster looks good. Maybe I just want to see what I've been missing."

"Okay."

We take a table that's been freshly cleared and cleaned. A waiter comes over and offers us menus. She says "We won't be needing those. We already know what we want."

"Want to hear the specials?"

"No, we're fine. Thank you. Fried oysters for me. And for my husband, the breakfast sandwich with, and I think I'm right, scrambled eggs, and grits," and I nod. "And the bacon extra crisp, if you can, and the eggs in the sandwich well-done, not loose."

"Right," I say.

"Anything to drink?"

"Café au lait for me," I say, "regular milk," and she says "Just water for me, please. From the tap. No ice in the glass or squeezed lemon, either."

"I think I can remember all that," and he goes into the kitchen. Then comes back a few seconds later and says to me "You did say you want the eggs in your sandwich scrambled, not fried or turned over."

"That's right. But scrambled till the eggs are almost overcooked."

"It's because of the fried oysters. I got the orders mixed up. Now I got it," and laughs and goes back to the kitchen.

"I'm a little wary what we'll end up with," she says, "but I'm sure it'll work out right." She takes my hand and kisses the knuckles. "This has been, despite the thought of the car accident, a day that I think I won't find unmemorable. Is that the right word?"

"What else could it be?"

"The day?"

"The word."

"*Unrememorable?*"

"No."

"Well, you're the writer, I'm the scholar. So we come out even, though in this case you're probably right."

"Probably? To be absolutely honest, I would just word what you want to say differently."

"What are we talking about? Boy, for someone as educated as I am, and in literature no less, I'm really having trouble with my native language today. Maybe it's the sun. My brain's been baked, driving with the top down. Anyway, what of it to whatever we've been talking about. We're happy, aren't we? Content. Together. This gorgeous day, weather-wise. 'Weather-wise'? And about to have what I think will be a delicious lunch."

"I'm sure it'll be delicious. And I couldn't be happier. I love you, my darling."

"Same with me for you." She squeezes my hand and lets it go. "And you're truly not angry with me for getting in that accident?"

"It's your car, and why would I even if it were mine. It'd be a bit of a nuisance, which it has been for you, that's all. Getting it fixed, getting the rental, dealing with the insurance companies. I wish I could have helped you out more with it, but you did everything better than I could ever do and in record time, and the accident wasn't your fault. You said so, the other driver did, and the police officer too. Was it a woman or a man?"

"The officer? A woman. Then a policeman came in another patrol car and did some measuring and more paperwork, and they both took my side."

"So why would you think there'd be a possibility of my being angry at you for it? The guy smashed into your car."

"That's what happened."

"You didn't smash into his. You were driving the way you're supposed to. You were always a much more careful driver than I. I'm just thankful you weren't hurt. And he wasn't too. And that he didn't get mad at you, screaming, raving, making a scene. Blaming it all on you. Even threatening you, which can happen."

"He didn't. He was very calm and apologetic and blameworthy. I can say it that way, can't I?"

"Sure, why not? So I'm glad it worked out peaceably for you and relatively easy too. That everyone cooperated in not making it a worse experience than it was."

"Now you're the sweet one."

"What do you mean?"

"Well, before—in the car, I think. Yes, it was in the car. Where else could it have been if it was just before and not here?—you called me sweet. Or said I was sweet."

"I don't remember. But if you say I did, then I did. I'll always take credit for doing a nice thing. And I'm glad I called you sweet, because you are sweet."

The waiter sets down in front of her a glass of water with a straw in it.

"You needn't have given me a straw, but that's okay," and she takes the straw out of the glass and puts it on the table. "And the coffee?"

"It's being prepared."

"No rush," I say. "When it comes, it comes, just so long as it's still warm."

"That, except for the last part, is my husband's philosophy. Never get excited."

"That's not a bad one," the waiter says. "I ought to adopt it." He picks up the straw on the table. "Your coffee should be ready now and possibly your food too," and he goes into the kitchen.

"I get excited over some things, but probably not the way you mean," I say. "Selling a story to a major magazine. Selling a book, or just having a good publisher take it. Getting an award or honor of some kind for my work, especially when there's some money attached to it. And also when one of the kids has some kind of achievement. Getting into a top college of their choice. Both of them. I remember, with the first one, when the envelope arrived and she opened it, expecting rejection, though I knew by the size of the envelope that it could only be good news. And she read the first line of the letter and smiled and I asked her what the letter said. I cried I was so excited. And things that happened with you. Not just when you said you'd marry me. And of course in the hospital when we had our babies, but when you got the job here and that fellowship for your translation work and then tenure. I was excited all those times."

"I know."

"I get excited sometimes even when the dentist tells me at the end of my semiannual checkup, and probably because it rarely happens, that my teeth are fine and he'll see me in six months, not the following week because of some new cavity."

"I don't know why I said it. And I used the wrong word. I should've said 'rattled,' which you never get, at least around me. I don't even know if that would have been the right word to use. But let's drop it, my sweet unrattleable husband. I think we've been talking about two different things."

The waiter comes with our food and my coffee. "Anything else I can get you folks?" and she says "I don't think so," and he goes. I've been crying a little, feel it most in my throat, tried not to show it and dab with my finger whatever might be around my eyes.

"Oh, you're something," she says, and pats my hand.

"I'm sentimental, that's all. You must think I'm acting foolishly."

"Of course I don't. Though if the waiter saw it, he could have thought... well, who knows what he could have thought. Let's eat, shall we?"

She puts a fried oyster on my plate and a little of that white sauce that comes with it. It has a name but I forget what it is. Not "cocktail." I count the fried oysters left on her plate and the one on her fork. Four, and they're not very big. I hold up the plate with my sandwich on it and she shakes her head. "Not even half of a half?—I can cut it for you," and she says "Really, I've enough and have had my eggs for the day. Maybe even for the week."

We eat without saying anything to each other. I want to say something but don't have anything to say. I don't know why she doesn't say anything. Maybe for the same reason. We just eat and drink and look around the restaurant or out the window or stare into space. Finally, when we're done eating, I say "Anything on your mind?"

"Nothing, as usual. But that was delicious and just enough. If I'd had more I might not be looking forward to them the next time I'm here."

"You mean you're already thinking of ordering them the next time you come here?"

"If they're on the menu. If not, something else. Everything's good here. How was your sandwich? You ate it all and the tartar sauce too. Do you want the rest of mine? You can smush it around the lettuce the oysters came on."

"Are you being funny?"

"No, serious. The sauce was also special but they gave too much."

"No, thanks. And the sandwich was good. Delicious. And so big. I ate more of it than I should have. And with the grits? I'm stuffed."

"And the fried oyster?"

"That's what put me over the top. It wasn't big, but it was rich, and good. My very first, I think. I can't remember ever having one before."

"At your department's end-of-the-academic-year party for the grad students and staff. You must have tasted one there. They were much smaller, though, and also served with tartar sauce."

"I always thought they were fried clams. But oysters?"

"Oysters. Several times. I don't ever remember fried clams at it."

"Anyway, they couldn't have been as good as you get here. If you have them here another time, and you say you will, and I'm with you, I won't refuse you if you offer me one. But only if you want to. So, ready to go? I wouldn't mind putting in a couple hours' work at home. I didn't get much done this morning, not that that's such a tragedy."

I signal for the check, get it, pay up, go to the men's room—I never leave a restaurant or movie theater or really any place I go to like that without going to the men's room first—and we leave the restaurant and get in the car. She starts it up, presses a button on her door and all her windows open. She plays with the button till all the windows are only half-open.

"Will it be too breezy for you?" she says.

"It's okay. We'll see while we're driving," and she pulls out of the parking space and we head home.

She starts smiling soon after we take off, not at me, but just looking out the windshield and it seems smiling to herself. I want to ask what she's smiling about, but think maybe it's better I don't. But I can't help myself. I want to say something and not stay silent. So I say "You haven't stopped smiling since we drove off from the restaurant. What's that all about?"

She cups her hand behind her right ear and stops smiling.

"You saying you can't hear me?"

"No, I can't."

"But you heard me just now?"

She cups the same ear with her hand and says "What's that you said?"

"Maybe it'd be better if we close all the windows. At least ours. Or try just closing the rear windows, or I'll just close my window," and I press what I think is the window button on my door. Nothing happens. I press the other end of the button and my window closes. "Can you hear me better now?"

"Not great. But what was it you were saying before that I couldn't hear or only got part of?"

"It's not important."

"Just tell me."

"Good. You can hear me now. You wouldn't think one closed window would do the trick. I was just wondering what it was you were smiling so much about before."

"I didn't get all of that, but do you mean in the car?"

"Yeah. Here. Was it anything about me?"

"Why would you think that?"

"That's what I was thinking too, but I couldn't help myself from asking it. Stupid, right? But we should probably save it for later when we get home. The car's not the most ideal place to hold a conversation in when you're having trouble hearing what the other person's saying. And I also don't want to take your attention away from your driving, especially in a car you're not familiar with. That's all right. Also wasn't important. I'm just talking to talk."

"That also I didn't quite catch. Talking for or about what?"

"Really, nothing. We'll finish the conversation, if we still want to, when we get home."

I look out my side window for most of the trip home. For the last few minutes of it I close my eyes and doze off. Next thing I know she's backing up the car into the carport and she turns the motor off. My car's in the driveway parked parallel to the carport. She taps my shoulder. "We're home."

"I know. I wasn't asleep. Just thinking."

"Maybe later you'll tell me what about."

"I'll probably forget by then. It wasn't a startling thought. Or illuminating. Or whatever I'm trying to say."

We get out of the car. I unlock the front door of the house and open it and the cat shoots out. "Should I get him?"

"It's okay. We have a couple of hours before it starts getting dark."

"Then I'm going in back," and she nods and I go to our bedroom to either write or nap.

THE LOST ONE

by STEPHEN DIXON

"GOOD MORNING, MY DEARIE. Sleep well?"

"I want to go home."

"I know," he says. "Not yet. And say 'good morning.' You don't have to say 'my dearie.'"

"You don't understand. Or you're not listening. I want to go home because I want to die there."

"I understand. But you're almost all better here. Then we'll go home."

"Stop playing with me. I'm never getting better. I might improve enough to be discharged. Then I'll be back in a month or two. Even a week or two. That's how fast it can happen. Each time I've come here has been quicker than the time before. I'll get double pneumonia again. Then they'll want to put a feeding tube in me again, but I won't let them. The trach's enough. I don't want another hole drilled in me. Don't be a dictator. You have to let me do what I want. But in my real bed or the stinking hospital bed at home, if that makes it easier for you to take care of me till I die."

"Come on, none of that. You'll be okay when you get home. We'll alternate between the hospital bed and our regular bed. Anything you want. Or just our regular bed. We'll rearrange all the machines we got there. I want you in that bed too. I want to sleep with you at night. Just give it a few more days."

"Please, get it into your head. I don't want anything done for me anymore. It's a farce. I'm done being part of it. I'm either going to starve myself to death here or in the hospice they ship me to or at home. Isn't it better for all of us if it's at home?"

"Whew, what a way to start the morning. Let me get my coat off. And have my coffee and bagel before they get cold, and then we'll talk."

"Don't try to get out of it. If you don't start the process this minute for me to leave here, I'll ring for the floor nurse to. Or the social staff or whoever they are. You know; we've dealt with them the last times. For them to arrange for me to go home. Are you going to do it? If not and you won't let me ring for the nurse, I'll scream for someone to come help me."

"Oh, Jesus, how I hate this."

"You don't think I don't? But what can we do? Take off your coat, ring for the nurse, and then have your bagel and coffee."

He speaks to the people he has to to get her discharged. Calls their daughter and says "Don't bother coming to the hospital. We're on our way home." A nurse and he get her dressed and all her things in two shopping bags. An ambulance comes, she's put on a gurney and wheeled downstairs and driven home. The ambulance gets there before he does in his car.

"Good, you're here," she says, still lying on the gurney. "They don't know where to put me. They think the hospital bed. I'd like to start off for a day or two in our bed. Then you can do what you want with me. But you should call that medical supply service to get all their stuff out of the hospital bed room by the time I end up there. If you want to replace it with flowers, I wouldn't mind. The room should be more cheerful-looking and smell better."

The ambulance people get her into bed and then leave.

"Can I get you anything?" he says to her. "Water? Something to eat?"

"Nothing. Thank you. But isn't this better, having me home? I know I'm happier."

"No, nothing is better. Everything's miserable."

"Daddy, don't," their daughter says. "It doesn't help matters."

"It's okay for your father to say what he wants. For both of you to. I know what you're going through. It isn't easy for me either, of course. But believe me, I do feel better, being home. I know I did the right thing. And our little pussycat seems happy to see me and I'm happy to see him, so that's a big plus too. They never would have let him visit me in the hospital."

"They would've in the hospice," their daughter says. "They asked us to look at a few."

"That's the best thing I heard about them, but who'd want to go there? Nothing beats being home. Listen, though," she says to him. "Just so I don't forget or am unable to bring it up later. After I'm gone—"

"Stop talking like that," he says.

"Why? This is important. After I'm gone I want you to start leading a normal life again. To go out; to meet someone. Don't say no to any dinner invitation or parties and such. Friends wanting to introduce you to a woman they think you might like. I'm saying: after a while. I don't want you to be lonely. It isn't healthy. Be realistic. You're still a good catch and I'm not the only one you could love. What was I, the fifth? The sixth? Just the longest. Promise me you'll do what I say. That'll make me feel better too."

"I can't think about it. It's the furthest thing from my mind. Don't be cruel to me."

"Daddy. That's not nice."

"It's all right. I know what your father means. I'm sorry," she says to him. "Maybe I was wrong. Hold my hand?"

He pulls up a chair beside her and sits and holds her hand. She smiles at him and he just stares back. "I'm so sad. I can't hold it in," and he starts crying. Their daughter starts crying. "Look what I've done," he says.

"Look what I've done, you mean," she says. "But it's okay. Crying's good for us. We have a good reason to. Give me a kiss, everybody?"

They kiss her. Their daughter says she'll go out for flowers for the whole house. He says "Use my credit card we share. Also, go to the market and get lots of special prepared foods, for lunch and dinner."

"Not for me," his wife says. "I'm on a diet," and she laughs.

"Just a little? Smoked salmon. Not the packaged lox but the freshly sliced kind from their fish counter. One of their prepared soups—lobster bisque; anything. Or just split pea, which'll be easier on your stomach. And chocolates. Strawberries. Those miniature crab cakes. It'll be like New Year's Eve. You have to. One last time. No, forget I said that. Not the last time. Maybe you'll like it so much you'll want to have more tomorrow and the next day and the day after that. Please? We'll be very careful when we feed it to you. Tiny bites. Long waits between them. And champagne tonight. I've got a great bottle I'll put on ice."

"A little, then, but not of everything. Just to satisfy you. Though I have to admit the smoked salmon and champagne and strawberries sound nice. All I had at the hospital went straight into my arms."

"And what do you say to breakfast tomorrow? Hot cereal. A scrambled egg?"

"That's going too far."

They go to bed late the first day she's home and he holds her all night from behind. "Thanks," she says. "This is worth everything." They sleep together the second night, same way, till she says her right side hurts and she wants to be on her back. He turns her over on her back and she falls asleep with his hand on her shoulder. Next morning she says "I think I should move to the hospital bed tonight. I'll miss you. But I spoke to a hospital nurse about this before I left, went over all of it, and it seems I'm going to start making a mess in the bed in the next couple of days, so let it be in my own bed. If you mind the cleanup, the nurse also said our health insurance probably covers calling in a home aide to help with things like that a few hours a day."

"I know about it. But our sweet child and I will do everything. My mother and I did it with my father for more than a year. Of course I won't have Rosie do the grungier stuff. That'll be me. And you understand why I don't want an aide. I don't want anybody else around."

From the first day he's arranged for a home hospice nurse to look in on her twice a day. Blood pressure, lungs, check for bedsores. The nurse says "She's surprisingly chipper, for all she's gone through and still has to face. Was she always that way?"

"Mostly. But I think now she wants to make it easy as can be for our daughter and me."

"I'll pray that it lasts till she goes into her final coma."

After the nurse leaves that third morning, she says "Did she come with the morphine this time? I don't know how they could forget such an important thing two days in a row."

"Don't worry, she brought it. Several doses. They only give so many at a time. If for some reason I'm running out of them, they can run a new batch over here in less than an hour, no questions asked."

"Do you know how to use it?"

"It's so simple. I used to give my father it, but then it was with a syringe. I had to be taught on an orange. Now, I just put it between your upper lip and gum."

"You sure? You'd think it'd go on the tongue. Call her cell phone to make sure. Things could change for me all of a sudden, and I want it to be right the first time."

"Take my word. It's between the upper lip and gum."

"I can't believe you're arguing with me. Just do what I say."

"I'm sorry, my darling, I'm sorry. This whole thing has weakened me. I'll call her this minute. If she doesn't answer, I'll get someone at the hospice who'll know."

The fourth night, he turns the radio on in her room to the classical music station. "Beethoven's violin concerto. It's a little schmaltzy. Do you mind?"

"It's all right. I can barely hear it. You listen to it," and she soon falls asleep. She cries out his name a few hours later. He's sleeping in the easy chair he brought into the room, and turns on the light. "What is it? You need changing?"

"I want to tell you this before I can no longer remember it. I know it sounds like a deathbed cliché, but I saw my parents just before. They were really there, at the foot of this bed. They told me not to worry. That no pain will come to me. That everything would be all right. It's true. It happened."

"I believe you. It must have made you very happy and given you some relief."

"It did. Both. I can even tell you what they were wearing. And my father was holding his hat."

"Do. Tell me. I want to hear everything."

In the morning she opens her eyes and says "Hi. It must seem like I've been asleep till now, but I haven't. I've been memorizing a poem that came to me in a dream. It's a poem of thanks to our cat. How protective he's been of me all these years I've been sick. Would you write it down for me?"

"I'll get a pen and pad."

She dictates a short poem to him and then looks up at the ceiling and smiles.

"Is it finished?"

"For the moment."

"It feels finished as a poem."

"Then maybe it is. Unless more of it comes to me today, in or out of sleep, that I want to add to it. But I don't think anything will."

"Did a title for it also come in your dream?"

"Not that I can remember. You give it. Though if you want, call it 'A Poem of Thanks.'"

A few hours later her eyes open and her lips are moving. He says "Do you want to speak?"

"I'm still thinking," she says.

Her best friend in Baltimore comes to say goodbye. Later, he tells her "Other people want to visit you. I get calls. Some from New York."

"Tell them no. You say goodbye for me. Everybody will understand. It's become too sad for me. It's not that I know I must look like a wreck."

"You look fine. Really you do."

She shuts her eyes and scowls.

That night she wakes up and says "There you are. I thought I lost you. You know what? I think I'd like to start getting ready for the day."

"What do you mean?"

"That's all I meant. I'm not being complicated."

She doesn't wake up the next morning. He says her name softly and their daughter says "Mommy, are you awake?" She doesn't move.

"She must be in a coma. That's what my father looked like when he went into one. He stayed in the same position for two days. With my mother, though, she was in and out; in and out. Then she just opened her eyes wide, sat up and regurgitated a lot of horrible fluid from her stomach and died. I was the only one in the room."

She's in a coma for two days when he says to his daughter "I can't stand it anymore. I don't want her to suffer. I certainly don't want her to die. I want to get her back in the hospital and on IVs. We did this too fast. I'm sure she can get well again."

"What are you saying? Are you crazy? The nurse said yesterday her kidneys have stopped functioning. Maybe a lot worse has gone on in her body since she's been home. There's no bringing her back. I'm sure they won't even take her. This is what she wanted. If by some miracle she was able to be revived and could speak or make herself known in some way, she'd hate you because she'd just have to go through all this again. Go out for a walk, Daddy. Take your mind off her for an hour. If anybody needs to, it's you."

"Okay, I'll walk. And I'll walk and I'll walk. Look after her while I'm out and consider what I said about getting her back in the hospital."

"Go, Daddy. Take your walk."

She's in a coma for nine days. She seems to be in pain sometimes. Winces; jerks her head; makes a growling noise. "She looks it, doesn't she?" he says to their daughter. "I can't tell for sure. What do you think? The morphine certainly can't hurt her, even if we're giving her more than they said we should."

They take turns sitting by her bed, recounting pleasant and funny events for her and reading poetry aloud from several books. "Do you think this is any use?" he says.

"It might not look like it, but she hears us. Hearing's... well, you know as well as I do. I bet if you pricked her with a needle, she wouldn't react to it. But if we shouted, she would, though I don't want to test it. So let's make sure every poem we read to her is beautiful and clear and all the family memories we tell her are also clear and happy. I want her to enjoy it as much as she can."

The next morning he says to his wife "I'm going to read to you now from a huge anthology of Chinese verse. You know the one. Three thousand years of it. It's your book. You had it when I first met you. It was always in that tall, narrow built-in bookcase to the left of the living room windows overlooking Riverside Park. I remember it also as always being on the bottom shelf, the one level with the floor and for oversized books. I won't say who the poets are because I don't think I can pronounce their names right. I'll give their years, though."

He starts reading. A minute or so later her eyes open for the first time since she went into the coma, or the first their daughter or he saw, and then look blank. He yells "Rosie, come here. I think Mommy's succumbing." He tries to close her eyes but they won't close easily and he doesn't want to force them. They sit on either side of her for a few minutes without saying anything and then he says "I know she's gone. You think so too, right? The poor dear. But no pain. Thank goodness for that. But I think I should call the hospice now."

"Do you want me to do it?"

"No, I will. I know just what to say."

He calls and says to the woman who answers "I think my wife died. No, she definitely did. We get a nurse from you twice a day under home hospice care, to look in on her. Can one come right away to confirm her death? Because then I have to call the funeral home to get her over to the National Institute of Health—I think that's it—near DC, to do some work on her. An autopsy. Her brain and such. For medical research of her disease. It's all been prearranged. I know I sound stilted and a little confused. I should have had my daughter call you. But they said I shouldn't take too much time getting my wife there. NIH did. That time is of the essence. All right? You have my address?"

A nurse comes an hour later. The one who came most of the time. They go into his wife's room. "It's what you said," she says. "Just looking at her I can tell. My deepest sympathy, sir and miss. I'll do the various tests on her because I'm required to and call them in to her GP to get his authorization. Then we should all pray."

"We don't pray here. Oh, maybe my wife did and I didn't know about it. She was very interested in religious studies, though I know it's not the same thing. And maybe my daughter does and I don't know it. But I don't."

"Daddy! Enough. And I'll pray for Mommy. If I'm going to pray once in my life, what better time than now?"

The nurse examines his wife, writes some things down on a couple of sheets of paper, goes outside and sits in her car and makes some calls on her cell phone, comes back and gives him a copy of one of the sheets and tells him to give it to the funeral home, and then she and his daughter stand by the bed and close their eyes and pray.

He calls the funeral home. Then says to the nurse and his daughter "They're on the way. Now everyone has to leave the room. I want to wash her and get a fresh gown and pad on her."

"I'll help you," his daughter says.

"No. You've done enough. More than enough and have been a great help. But Mommy wouldn't want me to let you do this. I spoke about it with her."

The funeral people come and he helps them get her into a body bag on a gurney. She's wheeled outside. It's a truck they came in, not a hearse. "You know where to take her?"

"We have thorough instructions," the driver says.

"What happens after?"

"NIH contacts us and we bring your wife to the funeral home and she's cremated there, your ticket says."

His daughter and he stand outside and watch the truck pull away. "By the direction they took, I guess they're going to the beltway."

"You should eat, Daddy."

"I don't feel hungry. Later."

"Do you mind if I take the car to get a coffee and maybe something to eat?"

"Sure, take the car. I won't need it. I'm not going anywhere. And I'll be all right alone here. I don't know how I'm going to live without her, but I'll be fine. Not quickly, but in time. Both of us, of course. I feel so strange. Don't you? Such a tough thing to sink in. Or something. I think I'll in fact nap."

The funeral director calls two days later. "We brought your wife back from NIH this morning. If you want to view the body before she's cremated, you can do it anytime today before six p.m."

"Me? See her? I couldn't. She'd be so disfigured."

"I didn't think you would, but we always have to ask. Your daughter? Should I assume the same?"

"I'm sure she also won't want to, but I'll mention it to her. Or maybe I won't. She might think it's her duty to go—that one of us should—and I wouldn't want her to. But you'll call me when it's over to pick up the cremation container, right?"

"Since there's no ceremony planned, we can deliver the container to you. You're only fifteen minutes away."

"No, I'll come get it. I could use the break. I haven't been out of the house for two days. I might even... Nah, I was going to say I could come with my daughter and go out for lunch with her after, but I don't think I'm ready for that yet."

His daughter suggests they hold a memorial either here or in New York. He says "I doubt your mother would have wanted one, though I never talked about it with her, and I don't need it, do you?"

"It'd be for friends and colleagues here. And in New York for friends and our relatives there."

"Then have one if you want. Both places, even. That wouldn't be that unusual, I'd think. I'll take care of all the expenses. Flowers, refreshments, rental of the places you have it in. But I won't be there."

"Then we won't have one. And I better start thinking about flying home soon. You said you'd be all right. You seem better. But I won't, or not immediately, if you don't want me to go."

She flies back to San Diego a few days later. They talk on the phone every night. One time he cries on the phone. She says "Want me to visit you this weekend, Daddy? For now it's all the time I can afford."

"Hold off for a while till you have more time and it pays for you to come. I'll pay your airfare. And of course I'm not saying it wouldn't be wonderful to see you. But it's not necessary for my sake. I'm good. Really, so much better. So not to worry."

"Then how about you coming here for a week or so?"

"Me? Travel? The airport? Not sleeping in my own bed? Not now, my darling. Maybe one day."

For a few weeks neighbors and former colleagues of his leave food and flowers and a little plant by the kitchen door. If he hears the doorbell and he's in back, he doesn't answer it. If he's in the kitchen and sees a car pull up or someone walking along the driveway to his house, he goes in back. They probably know he's here because his car's here, he thinks, or maybe they'll think he's gone out for a walk. Once when he's on his knees swabbing the kitchen floor, a neighbor knocks on the door and gives him what he brought. It's on a dinner plate, in aluminum foil. "This is the third time I brought this down today. I didn't want to leave it. Thought the raccoons might get it first."

"Yeah, they can be quite the rascals. Dogs too. Thanks very much. Everyone's been so kind. And please thank your wife. I'm sure I'll like it, whatever it is. And take the plate because I don't know when I'll return it."

He gets lots of condolence cards and some letters. Also confirmation notices of donations people made to an organization that provides funds for research of her disease and of trees planted in Israel, all of them in his wife's name. He doesn't answer any of the letters or cards. Tries to but breaks down after a sentence or two and gives up on it. As for the donators, he can't think of anything appropriate to say and some of them he doesn't have their addresses. If he sees them or speaks to them on the phone he'll thank them. He thinks he'll remember who they are. Just in case, he makes a list of all their names, with a "DR" or "DT" next to the ones that made donations. Some of the cards and letters make him cry because of what they say about his wife and, in a few of them, the way he took care of her for so long. Two of the letters he doesn't know what the writers mean. All the letters are handwritten.

He puts the cremation container in the garden shed. His daughter and he were undecided what to do with it. About a month later he sees it there. He can't just leave it in the shed, he thinks. The weather or something will get to it, since it's only made of heavy cardboard, though it's sealed tight. He was told at the funeral home when he ordered it that once the lid's shut it's impossible to open the container without destroying it. He buries it under the star magnolia tree right outside the house. His wife had him plant the tree there more than ten years ago. It was her favorite tree on the property, though she wished its flowers would last longer than two weeks. It was around three feet tall when he planted it. She had ordered it from one of the garden catalogs she got through the mail regularly. Now it was around twelve feet. He thinks he'll have a tree service cut down the branches of another tree hanging above it, or maybe just have that tree removed. That'll also bring a lot more light into the house.

He trades in their custom-made handicapped van for a much smaller car. They only had the van for three years. He doesn't get much for it. The salesman says "It's badly scratched, outside and in, and will need a complete paint job. Even then, because it's a special-needs vehicle, it'll probably still sit on the lot for months before anyone's interested in it." He knows he could get more for it if he advertised it in the *Baltimore Sun* and local *Pennysaver*. But he doesn't want to go through all the hassles of that and exchange the handicapped license plates for regular ones and pay insurance for both cars till he sells the van. He has to do something to make life easier for himself, even if it costs him.

He donates all his wife's clothes to AMVETS and Purple Heart. He first offers them to his daughter. She says "Mommy and I weren't the same size in anything but shoes. And she herself told me it's not good for the feet to walk around in someone else's shoes even if the two people are the same size."

"But you'll take her jewelry, what little she had, next time you're here? Not her wedding band. That and mine and maybe even her parents' marriage rings, if I can find them, I'll turn in for cash, though whatever I get for them I'll give to you."

"She had beautiful jewelry. But I'd be afraid I'd lose some of it or it'd be stolen. Nona's pearl necklace, especially, she got from her father after Nona died, and the amber-beaded one you gave her as an engagement gift. I also wouldn't feel right wearing anything of hers. Too spooky. So do what you want with them."

"That's my point. I've no idea what to do with them. I guess, for the time being, they'll just have to stay in her dresser drawer. But they could be stolen from there too."

"Rent a small safe-deposit box at the bank for them."

"Then I'll never see them again, for I have nothing else to put in the box, and you'll be stuck with them after I go."

"Don't talk like that. Not even in fun."

For several months he refuses all dinner invitations from friends and offers by some of them to go to the theater or a concert or movie with him. In a letter to a friend in Maine he writes about this. The friend writes back "The same thing that happened to me after Hannah died will happen to you. Keep turning down these invites and you'll stop getting them."

"About my turning down invitations," he writes back, "you're no doubt right. But it still feels impossible for me to go anywhere special without my dear wife. When the time comes and if the invitations haven't all dried up, I'll start accepting them and possibly even make my own invitation calls."

He invites for dinner at his house the couple his wife and he were closest to. They'd invited him a number of times for dinner or just to meet someplace for lunch or coffee. He always gave them one excuse or another for not going, but didn't want to lose them as friends. If he does break down in front of them, he thinks, that'll be okay. They're the one couple he can do that with without being embarrassed by it. He starts off with two appetizers he made, which he always used to do, and opens a good bottle of wine. Interesting conversation, some laughs. A month later, while his daughter is visiting him, the couple invite them to dinner at their home.

"I had them here," he says to his daughter, "and it went fine. I didn't choke up once. So now I think it's time for me to step out. That is, if you don't mind going. I don't think things have improved with me that much where I could go alone."

"I'd like to go. I like them very much, and they loved Mommy."

They're having drinks in the living room of the couple's house when he sees on a bookshelf a small framed photo of his wife. "That's new," he says to them. "I don't recall the photo."

"Lunch here years ago on the patio," the wife says. "A Labor Day weekend, just before we all began the fall semester. Both John and I claim to have taken it. But I'm sorry. I didn't think. Does it disturb you? I could remove it."

"No, I like it, and that you thought so much of her that you put it there next to your kids' photos. And she looks great. So happy. Not at all sick."

During dinner, every time his wife's name is mentioned or something the two couples did together comes up, he feels he's about to cry. Could be the wine influencing him, he thinks. He's had a lot. He even has to excuse himself from the table one time and go into the kitchen to cry. And then to the bathroom, when the crying becomes sobs, where he turns on the water in the sink so nobody will hear him. He thought he could cry in front of the couple, if it came to that, but not this much.

His daughter drives them home. He feels too shaky and also a bit too tired to. He says in the car "I've made a decision. I'm not going to anyone's house for dinner or drinks or anything like that again for a while, even if you're here and offer to come with me. Nor meet anyone but you for coffee or lunch outside the house. You saw. It's still too difficult for me. I don't know why it was different when I had them over for drinks, but it was. Of course, the photo of your mom there didn't help.

"They meant well."

"No, I'm not saying they didn't. It's my problem alone. But you wonder."

"You wonder what?"

"You wonder, you wonder. How long does it keep up? I've photos of her all over the house, and I live with them just fine."

When they get home he thinks maybe he should put away some of the photos of his wife. He has so many out. One on his bedroom wall, another on the dresser. Others are on a bookshelf in what was her study. Another's on the fireplace mantel in the living room. It's from her first year in college. Orientation week, she said, or parents' weekend; she forgets. She's lying on the grass in front of her dormitory, petting her pet gerbil, Myrtle. Several photos are held to the refrigerator door by magnets. One of them is of her and her mother and their daughter, taken in a topiary garden about a half hour's drive from their house. Only one of all these photos has him in it. At the outdoor wedding in Maine of their daughter's former babysitter there. His wife's in a wheelchair; he's standing behind her holding the chair's handles. They both look like they're having a good time. The photo he likes best out of all the ones he has displayed in the house is on the bedroom windowsill opposite his work table. It's about five by seven inches and is in a plexiglass frame. She never looked more beautiful and serene. Well, that's what he thinks. It was taken a year or two after she was diagnosed with her disease. She showed no signs of it, though. Only her vision was a little affected and she had a slight tingling in her fingers that came and went. He took the photo. She's sitting on the arm of an easy chair and smiling at the camera. She's in the left side of the photo. The main part of it has several children around a table watching their daughter blow out the candles on her birthday cake when she was six. It was in their apartment in New York on Riverside Drive. They kept the apartment after they moved to Baltimore when he got a teaching job there. They were eventually evicted from the apartment because the landlord proved it wasn't their main residence. They only stayed there most of June and a few weeks around winter break and for many week-ends—sometimes long weekends—and a week during spring break, when they'd take their daughter out of school if her Easter vacation didn't come at the same time as his spring break. She looks so healthy in the photo. But over the next few years she gradually got worse and then, about five years after that birthday party, she rapidly declined. She was in a wheelchair the last ten years of her life. No, longer. Fifteen.

"I'm going to die from my disease," she once said.

"No, you won't," he said. "I won't let you. And scientists are making great progress in finding cures for it."

"I hope it happens soon."

"The scientific breakthroughs, you mean."

"Of course. What else? Not my dying, that's for sure."

FINDING
AN ENDING

by STEPHEN DIXON

I CAN'T SEEM TO finish the story I've been writing. I've tried many times. So, try another time. That's the only way to do it. And if that doesn't work, then another time and another time till you've got it. You're so close to ending the story, end it already, add it to the collection of interlinked stories you've been writing, and start a new one.

She says "So I'll see you," and heads for the door. "Wait," he says and she says "What?" And he says "You forgot..." Forgot what? Her keys? Wallet? Shoulder bag? A book? Her briefcase filled with... Filled with what? What does it matter what it's filled with? Just her briefcase. Then, or... Better start again. This happens. I'm not worried. Somewhere out there's the right ending. It always comes. Or forty-nine times out of fifty it does. I just don't want all I've written so far of this story to go to waste. How many days have I been writing it to reach the point I'm stuck at now? Days. A week and a day, to be exact. Started it on a Sunday. Today's Monday. I remember that Sunday. I met someone for lunch. Allen and his son Ned. At the Village Square Café. And I drove back home and got the idea for the

story. It just popped into my head, and because I'd finished a story
the previous day, I was looking for a new story to write. Actually,
I got the idea for the story while I waited for Allen and Ned to show
up at the restaurant. They were about twenty minutes late—traffic,
they said; an accident on 83—and I jotted down several lines in the
little notebook I always carry in my back pants pocket and immediately went to my typewriter after I got home and peed and spooned
some cat food out for the cat, and wrote the first draft in one sitting.
Took me about half an hour. Came to six pages. And it won't be lost.
Not if I keep working on it. Though if it has to—if I try for another
day or two, but really put some time into it, and can't come up with
an ending—I'll just have to accept it. I've written so many stories.
Hundreds. Five hundred, six hundred; maybe more. I stopped counting around ten years ago. So a few unfinished stories, or one more
unfinished one, shouldn't matter that much. It shouldn't, but for a
little while it probably will. It's been about five years since I worked
on a story and couldn't finish it, though I got very close with that
one. I remember how lousy I felt at not being able to finish it. The
story's called "Sonya." I think before it was called "A Woman He
Met." It is based on the first time my future wife and I met. In the
story it's at a wedding reception in someone's apartment in New
York. In real life it was on a subway heading north on the Broadway
line. A local. I think I got on at 34th Street and she got on at 42nd.
I felt it too contrived, or maybe just hard to believe, or maybe I just
couldn't pull it off right, for them to first meet that way. Too much
like a movie. She was holding two bulky packages—they turned out
to contain a lamp and lampshade—in the crowded subway car.
I offered her my seat. "No, I couldn't," she said, and I said "Please,"
and stood up. Seated, and now I was standing in front of her, she
offered to hold my book—"It looks heavy." "That's all right," I said.
"I like holding it. It's like my security book, and you've got enough
on your lap." "I won't steal it," and I said "I know that." "May I see
what you're reading," and I showed her the cover. "Oh, yes," she said,

or something like it, indicating, I thought, that she was familiar with the book or author. "You know his work?" I said, and she nodded. "This one?" I said, surprised, because he wasn't a well-known writer in America at the time—Austrian; still alive then. Three short novels published in translation by a small press in Colorado. "No, a book of poems," and I said "I didn't know there was one. In English?" "Both. Face to face." "The book jacket doesn't say anything about his poetry. Nor does the introduction, or as much as I read of it. They're always too scholarly and a little too dry for me. Too much like literary criticism, while I'm more interested in the bio. So I mostly save them for if I'm uncertain about the plot and who's who and to whom and so on and I think I need some expert's take on it." "That's what I do," she said, "but the other way around. I write those literary criticisms, but not of his work." "Oh, I'm sorry," I said. "I didn't mean that pejoratively," and she said "I know. And I didn't take it as such." She smiled, took a book out of her coat pocket and started reading it. I wanted to ask what it was but didn't. I felt I'd talked enough for the time being and it turned out all right that I didn't ask. In both real life and story, they left together. In real life because it was their subway stop—116th Street. When we got out of the station I carried one of her packages: the one that contained the lamp; I insisted. And we were going the same way: I made sure she knew that. I didn't want her to think I was going out of my way for her, though now I don't know why I thought that. If it wasn't true, I could have given her a good excuse. We passed a coffee shop on Broadway and I said "Like to pop in here for a coffee?" and she said "Sure, why not? I could use a pick-me-up and also one of their delicious schneckens." In the story they talk for about an hour at the wedding reception. She has to leave it early to go to a concert at Lincoln Center. He says it's a good time for him to leave too. "I don't know anyone here but Hesh, we called him—the groom. We go all the way back to City College together but sort of lost contact till we bumped into each other on the street last week and he invited me to the wedding reception.

I guess he wanted someone here from his old days at City and I thought what the heck: I haven't been to a party in a long time and, truthfully, I thought I might meet someone at it." "City's where my ex-husband went," she says, "but probably a few years after you." "Do I look that old?" and she says "Just older than he. I was in graduate school with the bride." He walks her to the subway. "It might be out of my way, but so what? I like to walk." He asks and she gives him her phone number and last name and he writes them down in his memo book. He calls her the next day and they make a date for coffee at the same place my future wife and I went to that day we met on the subway: The Roasted Bean. It didn't last long—rent got too high—which was a pity because their coffee and coffee drinks and pastries were superior to any of the other coffee shops in the neighborhood. It's a pretty long story, making it even tougher to give up. More than twenty typewritten pages at a time when all my stories were a single paragraph. I put it in a file folder with the dozen or so other stories I was unable to finish, a couple of them going back almost fifty years. I thought one day, when I'd temporarily run out of ideas and opening lines for possible stories, I'd take the unfinished ones out of the folder, read them all and choose the one I thought had the best chance of finishing. If I couldn't finish it—and I doubt I'd put in that much time trying to: maybe a day—I'd try to finish the story I thought had the next best chance of being finished, and so on. I'm almost sure, after trying to finish three or four of them without any success, I'd give up on the rest of them and maybe even throw out the ones I worked on. "Sonya" I know I'll never throw out no matter how many times I'd try to finish it. It's a story very close to me—my wife really comes alive in it, things she says and does; some of what she says in it I even took word for word from journals she kept—and also because I put in more time writing what I have of it than the others. I don't think there's an unfinished story of mine I want more to finish. I even thought, as an experiment—I'd never done this in my writing—to retype one of these unfinished stories from the start, and if it didn't work with the first one I retyped, I'd try with another. I thought maybe by the time I got to where I left off in the story, an ending would come naturally either in my head or on the paper I'm typing, and with a little work I'd find a way to finishing it. I'm not being clear. Anyway, I never got a chance to work on even one of the stories in the folder, either by retyping it from the beginning or just concentrating on writing an ending to it. An idea for a new story, or the first line of one that started off an entire first draft, always came a day or two, or at the most, three, though it rarely took that long, after I finished a new story. The stories I wrote more than fifty years ago—maybe even fifty-five now—and couldn't finish, I threw out when I got a teaching job in Baltimore and moved down there. They were what could be called apprentice stories and weren't worth trying to finish because I knew they'd never be any good. In that plastic garbage bag of unfinished stories I left in front of the building I lived in before I moved to Baltimore were also all the poems and copies of them I'd written since I was twenty or so. I told myself I wasn't a poet and never was one. I was a fiction writer and I was only hurting my fiction by trying to do both. I also included in that bag a few one-act plays I'd written over the years and which later on I tried but failed to turn into short stories. By this time my future wife and I had been seeing each other for two years and we got married a year and a half after I started teaching and our daughter was born six months after that.

He says "Then we're through. Nothing more needs to be said about it. But I'm telling you, I've gone through this with other women I cared deeply about and it always hurt me, but I'm not going to let it hurt me again. So don't try to contact me after this unless you're thinking of resuming our relationship and you want to talk about it. Though if you do contact me for that, you better do it soon." No, too stiff. "Resume what we had going"? Not much of an improvement, and lots of other things wrong with it. "Gone through this" and "cared deeply about" and "not going to let it hurt me," and so on. And I've done a scene like that before in a previous story. Almost the same situation and what feels like the same words, if I remember right. I forget what story it was. Writing so many of them in more than fifty-five years, although the one I'm thinking of was fairly recent, there's got to be some repeats and maybe even repeats of repeats, not just in plots but in exact same lines. There seem to be only so many ways to say things in certain intense emotional situations like that. Maybe that's so. I'm not sure. In the one I'm thinking of, the couple—I think it's even called "The Couple"; it's from a ways back—have been seeing each other for about a year. Well, they met at a party at the end of November—the story follows pretty closely the timeline of the first summer together of my future wife and me—so a lot less than a year. They spent all of July and August in a cottage in Maine. A great place. About fifty feet through the woods to their own private cove by the ocean. She's a college teacher. Italian literature and language. He's a writer living off a small advance he got a few months before for a novel he's writing. Everything seemed to be going well between them. And the story might even have been called "The Cove." He was sure this was the woman he would eventually marry and have a child or two by. They hadn't spoken about it but it seemed she was as much in love with him as he was with her. They both had told each other so a few times. They hadn't had a fight or dispute of any kind that summer. In fact they hadn't had a fight or dispute or disagreement since they first met. He thinks he can say that. Her mother came up for a week in July and it went very well. Her father came up the last two days her mother was there and he got along very well with him. And his mother came up for a week near the end of their stay there and that also went very well. His mother said, when he was driving her to the Bangor airport, that she felt that Laura, the woman's name in the story, was like a daughter to her. "You couldn't have done better. Don't do anything foolish to lose her. You'll regret it your whole life." "I know," he said, "and I won't. It really looks good. She makes me so happy. It's hard for me

to even say that without tearing up. I think it's going all the way."
"That's what I like to hear," his mother said. During the drive back
to New York with Laura, they spoke about what a wonderful summer
it's been—the two of them, together, and also all the work they got
done. She said she never got along so well with any man for two
months straight and that includes her ex-husband before he was her
husband and at a time when she was madly in love with him. He said
"Same here. Never a summer like this or any two months straight
with a woman. Maybe not even two weeks. It's been a dream summer.
The cottage, you, your cats." The drive took ten hours. She sometimes took his hand for a few seconds while she drove or squeezed
his thigh and he did the same to her while he was driving. Lots of
loving smiles between them too in the car. And conversation. It was
all good, and for an hour or two they just listened to a book on tape.
She said something like "I'm all out of talk and not tired enough to
nap while you drive. Mind if I play one of the Hardy tapes?" He said
something like "Not my favorite writer, but go ahead. Anything you
want to make the trip go faster. And maybe it'll put you to sleep as
it would me if you were driving." "Now that's mean," she said. "I'm
sorry. I didn't mean it to be. Forget I said it." I don't remember which
Hardy novel it was. Maybe it was never mentioned. She had the
complete set of them on tape and also the collected poems. He
assumed she listened to the tapes when she was alone in the car
because she never played them when he was with her or even suggested she'd like to. The point is: it was a very pleasant ride back to
New York other than for that one Hardy remark. He knew Hardy
was one of her favorite writers. They stopped for lunch at a roadside
seafood stand in Massachusetts and shared a lobster roll and fish
burger and agreed they weren't as good as the ones at the Fish Net
in Blue Hill and the Fisherman's Friend in Stonington. So what
changed things when they got to New York? She must have been
thinking during the trip of breaking up with him or thought about
it long before, at least a few days before, while they were still in

Maine and, as far as he can remember, acting lovey-dovey to each other, but never gave a hint or sign it was on her mind or was something she had decided to do. All these thoughts of his come later in the story, near where I was unable to finish it, I think. She drove them to his apartment building on the Upper West Side, their first stop in the city. This was the arrangement they made in the car. First his place, then her parents', then hers. He never understood why and never asked her, or if he did he forgets what she said, why she didn't say goodbye to him for good while her car was double-parked in front of his building. It certainly would have been more convenient for him than to have to take the subway home after they got to her apartment. Maybe because she needed him to help bring her things up to her apartment while one of them stayed in the car if she couldn't immediately find a parking spot near her building or her parents'. That makes sense. Though her parents' building always had a doorman in the lobby who would have looked out for her car double-parked in front when she went upstairs. Her building also had a doorman, but she had so many more things to bring up to her apartment than he did to his, one of them being a very heavy electric typewriter and also a carton of books. He got out of the car, suspecting nothing, and brought his portable typewriter and other stuff he had with him in Maine to his apartment—clothes, manuscripts, writing supplies, flashlight, a few books, and jars of blueberry and raspberry jam for his mother and sister and a couple of friends and also to give as Christmas gifts when that holiday comes around. "I'll be right down," he said. "I just have to pee and drink a glass of water." She said "Try to make it fast. It's been a long trip for the cats and they're getting antsy in their carriers." Next they drove to her parents' apartment building near Riverside Drive about ten blocks north of his street and she brought their two cats back to them—he stayed in the car while she went upstairs. Then they drove to her building in the Morningside Heights neighborhood and brought the carrier with her two cats, all of them from the same family: mother and two daughters and son—to her apartment, along with lots of other things of hers. He actually helped her get everything of hers into the elevator and she went up with it and he rushed back to the car so she wouldn't get a ticket. The doorman had said he couldn't spend too much time looking out for the car. While she was in her apartment, or getting her things off the elevator and into her apartment, he drove around for about fifteen minutes looking for a parking space. He finally found one right in front of her building—it just opened up as he was passing her building for about the fifth time—and it was good for two days. How lucky can you get? he probably thought, or something like it. Once in her apartment—he had a key—he said "Well, that's done. And everything went so smoothly since we started out. Great journey, gorgeous weather, not one traffic tie-up, and perfect landing—I got a parking spot right in front of your building and it's good till eleven a.m. Wednesday. What better way to end the two best summer months I ever had." "I'm glad," she said, but after her face had changed. He means her expression. It had suddenly got so serious. He was expecting a smile from his last remark, maybe even a kiss. He said "Anything wrong?" "Why do you ask?" "Your face," he said. "You seem worried about something. You all right?" "Would you want to sit down and have some tea with me while we talk?" "Something is wrong," he said. "It's about me. I don't like it." "It's true," she said. "I hate spoiling your good mood, and this nice day, and so on, but this has to be said." "So come on. Out with it. You've already indicated it's no good. I did something you didn't like that I'm unaware of? Or I'm aware of it, though I can't for the life of me think what it could be, but you think I don't want to be reminded of it?" "No," she said. "Your parents? In Maine? But that was so long ago and I thought it went well with them." "It did. They had a wonderful time and think very highly of you. It's just that I've been thinking, but doing a lot of thinking about it because I know you're not going to like it." "The cats? You don't think I'm nice to them enough? And you feel, because as you once said they're part of the package, they'll never get along with me? I'm sorry. I shouldn't be joking." "I wish you wouldn't. But if you think it makes you feel better, since I'm sure you know by now what it is I want to tell you…"

I grab the story off my work table. In the unfinished stories folder? No, why bother? I'll never get back to it. And there are so many other more possible stories in the folder that I'll also never go back to or look at again other than maybe the first page or two and then probably dump. I tear the story in half and dump the pieces into the paper-recycling bag in the kitchen. I take a walk. I mow the grass. I take my pills. I feed the cat. I play with him a little while with a long strip of toilet paper. I drink a glass of water. I work out with weights. I run in place. I take a shower. I sit on the toilet and pee. I read today's newspaper while I have a couple of Bloody Marys. I make a sandwich. I eat half of it and throw the other half away. I drink a glass of wine while I sit on the porch and look out its windows. I watch a fox walk by. I stand up and wave my arms and yell "Get away, get away." I take one bite of a carrot and put the rest of it back in the refrigerator. I drink another glass of wine while I sit in the living room and listen to a baroque oboe concerto on the radio. I lock the doors and turn off all the house lights. I feel my way to the bedroom in the dark and turn on my bed lamp. I undress and get in bed. I get out of bed and brush my teeth and rinse my mouth with mouthwash and spit it out and clean the sink with my nailbrush. I pee. I read in bed. I look at my watch. I shut off the light and lie back in bed. I think: Why would you want to write another breakup story anyway? That could be the problem. You've done so many. They've for a long time been repeating themselves. You've for a long time been repeating yourself. There's nothing new for you to write about them. Face it: You've exhausted the subject. The subject doesn't excite you anymore, because you've exhausted it and you've got to be excited by what you write. If you had thought about this before you probably never would have written the last two or three of them. Is that so? That's so. I adjust the pillows behind my head. I pull the covers till they reach my neck. Tomorrow try to write an altogether different story, was the last thought I had before I fell asleep. I wake up in what seems like a few hours later. I turn on the light and look at my watch. Almost three hours exactly. I take my notebook off the night table, put on my glasses and write down the last thought I had before I fell asleep. Maybe it'll turn into the opening line to the first draft of a new story. You never know what's going to follow it and what it might lead to till you sit at the type-writer and type it out. I write that thought down also, change "type it out" to "write it down," and put the notebook, glasses, and pen back on the night table and shut off the light. I turn over on my left side and close my eyes. The cat jumps onto the bed and lies on my feet.

OH MY DARLING

by STEPHEN DIXON

HE GOES INTO HER room. The door was wide open and he just
slipped in. He's standing behind her and he doesn't want to startle
her. She might not know he's there. He just wants her to know what
happened to him. Maybe he shouldn't. She's busy. Reading on the
computer screen what she wrote and then typing some more. Or
maybe she knows he's there but wants to finish the sentence she's
typing before she loses it. Tell her later. Why's it so important she
should know now? No, tell her now. She'll see what it is the moment
she looks at him. But it's to get her to look at him that's the problem.
Try "a-hem." "A-hem," he says. First time he thinks he's used that
to get her attention. And in the thousands of pages he's written, he
doesn't think he ever used the expression once. She turns around to
him, wasn't startled. "Goodness, what happened to you?" she says.
"You mean the bruise on my forehead?" "More than a bruise. A cut."
"I fell again. Few minutes ago. Second time this week. A bad sign."
She turns back to the computer, shuts it off. "You shouldn't have
done that," he says. "You might lose track of what you were working

on. Your train of thought. What you were thinking to type. You know what I mean." "That's not as important as your head. Oh, my darling, I'm so sorry you fell. You took care of it? Washed it? Peroxide? Maybe it needs a dressing. It seems to have stopped bleeding." "The air will take care of it. A dressing—even a good Band-Aid—will just fall off." "You should call Dr. Anders, if you fell twice in two weeks." "One week," he says. "I will. Or think I will. But later. Not today. Now I've got a little headache from the fall and just want to rest. But I wanted you to know what happened. So you know I'm not holding anything back from you." She turns her wheelchair completely around to him and says "Come here," and spreads her arms out for him to come into them. He leans down and they hug. Then he gets on one knee and rests the non-cut side of his face on her lap. She rests her head on his. He goes into her room. Her study. It's always been "her study." Or has been for about ten years. Since she had the daybed taken out and a table with her computer on it and a bookcase with her books put in. They didn't use the room as a guest room anymore once their daughter graduated college and moved to New York. She's at the computer. He says "Excuse me." She turns around, says "Oh, dear," when she sees the bruise on his forehead. She asks what happened. He tells her. "Did you put peroxide on it? Wash it?" "I did everything," he says. "I took care of it, as they say. I didn't want to put one of those extra-large adhesive bandages we have on it because I think it'll heal faster exposed to the air. Maybe I'll put one on for when I go out so I don't horrify anyone with it." "You fell, you say, how'd you fall?" "I was just sort of propelled forward as if I was being pushed, and lost my balance and hit the bathroom door before I could stop myself with my hands out and bounced off it and fell to the floor. On the way down, unfortunately, I hit the sharp edge of the doorjamb." "Oh God, that's awful, and it could have been much worse. An eye. Your mouth." "That's what I thought too. I got off lucky you could say." "Are you going to call Milo about it? This is the second time you fell this month,

I think—maybe more you haven't told me about—although you never injured yourself like this." "No, two's all there are. And I will call Milo, I will, but not today, or maybe I won't tell him till my next checkup. It won't happen again. I'll be extra careful." "You don't want to chance it. It could be one of the medications you're taking. Something simple as that." "Don't I wish," he says, "but I doubt it." "What can I do but make suggestions? I'm sort of limited. I know I can't pick you up if you have another serious fall and can't get up by yourself. What I can do is give you a big hug. The cut—it looks more like a gash—seems to have dried." "It isn't a gash," he says. "If it was it'd still be bleeding. I'll take the hug, though." He comes into her study. She's typing away at her computer. She doesn't seem to have noticed he's there. "Excuse me for a second," he says. She continues typing, eyes focused on the screen. "Excuse me," he says louder, and she sort of jumps and stops typing and turns around to him. "You startled... oh my God, what happened to you? Your head." "Don't worry," he says. "It's nothing bad. I've taken care of it. You should have seen what it looked like before I cleaned it up. I fell. Tripped over my own foot and hit something hard. I looked for the box of large adhesive bandages, but we seem to be out. I wanted something to cover the mess so you wouldn't have to see it. It's okay now, but it left me with a fat headache. I wanted to tell you, though. I thought you'd be cross with me if I didn't. I should've waited till you were done with whatever you're working on there. I'm sorry." "You're sorry? Don't ever think that. Listen, we have to do something about your falling. This is the second time in the last month or so. That's two times too many. God forbid, if there's a next time, you might get hurt much worse." "Okay, we'll talk some more about it," he says, "and I welcome what you have to say, but right now I just want to rest my head." "Here, rest it on my lap," and she backs her wheelchair out from under the table and pats her lap. "I don't want to stain your dress if my head starts bleeding again." "Not to worry," she says. "It's denim and blood comes out easily with water or in the

wash. Just to be safe, though, not on the bruised side." "Maybe
I should just rest on the bed. It'll be easier. And I'll put a towel or
clean handkerchief on top of the pillow." "I'll come with you," she
says, and shuts down the computer and follows him in her chair. He
comes into her room. "Don't get alarmed," he says, "but something
awful happened." She turns around in her chair. "Oh dear," she says,
"what happened to your head? Are you okay?" "I am now. Before,
I wasn't too sure." "Is there anything I can do to help you?" "Nothing
I can think of. I think I took care of it. I fell again. I'm sure it's these
damn new running shoes I was stupid enough to let the salesman
convince me were the right size. I've always been an eleven- or eleven-
and-a-half-wide, never a twelve. The shoes are too large and the heels
move around too much no matter how tight I tie them and thick my
socks are. Wasted money. I'll take them off and never wear them
again, and they were expensive. I'm such a sucker to any authority,
even to a kid fifty years younger than me." "Don't blame yourself,"
she says. "We all make mistakes like that. You wanted to get out of
the store quick as you could because you hate shopping for things
like clothes. Here, come nearer. Let me look at it. Don't worry, I won't
touch it." He gets up close to her and bends his head down. "It looks
okay," she says. "Clean. You did a good job. Though it's a horrible
gash. You'll probably have another scar to add to the nine or ten
others you say you have on your head." "I was walking too fast.
Hurrying to the toilet because I suddenly had to pee, and tried to
correct the fall before I landed, and split my head open on the bathroom door. No, that's going too far, that 'split my head open.' I cut
it bad, that's all. Dented it you can say. My head, I mean, and just
maybe the door. I think I also hurt my right shoulder. But nowhere
near as bad. I also ended up peeing in my pants." "Do you want to
rest your head on my lap?" "I'd love to, but I might start bleeding
again. You know how the head is. I think for the time being I should
just stay standing or sitting upright without moving around too
much till I'm sure the cut's dry and there's even the beginning of a

scab over it." He goes into her room. "Something happened you might not like knowing about. Maybe I shouldn't be telling you, but you said you wanted me to if it happened again." She puts her hand over her mouth. "Nothing bad. Don't worry. Just bumped my head and hurt my shoulder. I know. Twice in two weeks." "One week." "One week then," he says, "not that it couldn't be two. What am I trying to say? I think the bump made me a little dopey. And it's really a coincidence the two falls were so close. Not a 'coincidence.' Another word. I'll find it. But I just have to be more careful from now on—slow down—but everything will be all right." "I hope so. And I'm glad you came in when you did. I have to be catheterized and was just about to call out for you. You'll be able to do it with your sore shoulder and head?" "Why not? And my shoulder's okay. I'll wheel you in back and get you on the bed." She turns off the computer. "You didn't want to print out what you had first?" "I won't lose it," she says. "And if I do, no great loss. I know where I am on it. And there's only one way of saying what I want to say in the part I'm up to in the essay, and it's mostly other writers' quotes." He wheels her into the bedroom, puts a towel down and lifts her out of the chair and gets her on her back on the bed. He takes off her pad and while he's catheterizing her she says "You know, you should tell Milo about your two falls." "It isn't necessary," he says. "And I have my semiannual checkup very soon. I'll tell him then, if I remember to." "Suppose you fall again before that? I mean, I hope not, but it could happen." "It won't. If it does, three in a short time is no coincidence, if they're the same kind of falls, though it might also just be one of the medications I'm taking or a combination of two or three of them. I have a sneaky suspicion that's it, but what do I know? But do you think we can have an end to this conversation?" "All right, I won't bug you on it anymore, at least for now." After he catheterizes her, he says "As long as you're on the bed and all this talk about catheterization—" "That's funny," she says. "It's all right with me, but what about your head?" "It feels better already," he says. He undresses her—everything but the long socks. He undresses, takes the phone receiver off its cradle and gets on the bed. He comes into the room. She's at her computer. "Hi," he says. "Hi," she says. "Oh, dear. You don't look so good. Your stomach?" "No, and it's funny you say my stomach," he says. "It's something entirely different." "So tell me, tell me. Come on, tell me." He comes into her room, wheels her to their bedroom, lifts her onto a towel on their bed, catheterizes her. "You know, you have a bruise on your forehead I didn't notice before or maybe it wasn't there. The left side, near the ear. From the same fall?" "If it's new, I guess so." "But your shoulder feels better?" "Better. And I didn't know about the bruise. Is it bad? Because I really took a fall." "You didn't see it in the mirror?" "I didn't look in the mirror." "It's more like a scrape," she says. "I'd put some A and D ointment on it if I were you." She turns to him as he comes into her room. "Oh, dear, what happened?" "What do you mean?" he says. "Your forehead. It's bleeding. Don't you feel it? Not heavily, but there's blood. Let me wipe it before it starts dripping to the floor." She takes a tissue out of a tissue box on her work table—"I'll do this very gently"—and dabs his forehead and shows him the tissue with his blood on it. "Honestly, I didn't know," he says. "I mean, I knew I fell but didn't think I hurt anything." "It isn't what you came in here for to tell me?" "No. I came in to ask if you'd be interested in taking a short break. Or not so short, but from your work." Comes into her room. She's working at her computer. "Damn," he says. "This is ridiculous. I came in here to tell you something but forget what it is." "Was it important?" "I think so. Or important as anything else is important." "It'll come to you. Maybe you just need to leave the room and retrace your steps from the time you first thought of coming in here. That might work." "I'll try it," he says. He leaves the room, goes back to their bedroom, sits at his work table there, takes the dust cover off his typewriter, puts it back on, gets up, and goes back to her room. She's working at her computer, looks up. "Well?" she says. "I did what you suggested. Felt like a fool doing it, but I still can't remember what I first came in here for." "Then it mustn't have been that important." "No, it was, or I thought so at the time. But maybe you're right. Sometimes I have a screw loose. That's not what you said but how I feel about myself. Does the same thing happen to you?" "Sometimes," she says, and turns back to her computer and starts typing.

ABANG is a visual artist based in Seoul. Her signature illustrations are fanciful and witty expressions of everyday life.

MARIE-HELENE BERTINO is the author of the novels *Parakeet* (a *New York Times* Editors' Choice) and *2 a.m. at the Cat's Pajamas* and the story collection *Safe as Houses*. Her work has received the O. Henry Prize, the Pushcart Prize, and the Frank O'Connor International Short Story Fellowship. Her fourth book, the novel *Beautyland*, is forthcoming from Farrar, Straus and Giroux.

KASHANA CAULEY is a writer for the television comedy *The Great North*, a former staff writer for *The Daily Show* with Trevor Noah, and a contributing opinion writer for the *New York Times*.

RITA CHANG-EPPIG received her MFA from New York University. Her stories have appeared in *Conjunctions*, *Clarkesworld*, *Kenyon Review* online, *Virginia Quarterly Review*, and elsewhere. She has received fellowships from the Vermont Studio Center, the Writers Grotto, and the Martha Heasley Cox Center for Steinbeck Studies at San Jose State University.

STEPHEN DIXON, a literary treasure and master of the short story form, died in 2019 at the age of eighty-three. One of the most prolific and innovative writers of his generation, he hammered away on a manual Hermes Standard until the very end, with, as he liked to say, "the two good fingers Parkinson's has left me." Dixon's remarkable six-decade career yielded thirty-five books (including the novels *I* and *End of I*, published by McSweeney's); nearly seven hundred published short stories; nominations for the PEN/Faulkner Award for Fiction and two National Book Awards; and multiple O. Henry Prizes, Pushcart Prizes, and appearances in *The Best American Short Stories*. His willingness to play with narrative structure, his lifelong dedication to creating something new in literature, and the fidelity with which he was able to reflect a real, lived life significantly influenced a generation of contemporary fiction writers. Two final collections of short stories (from which these four are drawn) and an authorized biography are due to be published next year.

JESSI JEZEWSKA STEVENS is the author of *The Exhibition of Persephone Q*.

GILLIAN LINDEN is a writer and English teacher. She lives in Brooklyn, New York.

ADAM ISCOE is a writer from Austin, Texas.

JON MCNAUGHT is a cartoonist, illustrator, and printmaker living in London. His latest comic book, *Kingdom*, was released by Nobrow in 2019.

MICHAEL KENNEDY is the author of the ongoing comic series *Mint*, and he illustrated the graphic novel *Tumult*. In addition to working as an editorial illustrator, he is currently working on two plays and his first novel. He lives in Birmingham, England, where he can be found reading *Nancy*.

ETGAR KERET, born in Ramat Gan, Israel, in 1967, is a leading voice in Israeli literature and cinema. Keret's books have been published in more than forty-five languages. His latest collection, *Fly Already*, won the most prestigious literary award in Israel, the Sapir Prize (2018), as well as the National Jewish Book Award from the Jewish Book Council.

POROCHISTA KHAKPOUR is the author of the novels *Sons and Other Flammable Objects* (Grove Atlantic, 2007) and *The Last Illusion* (Bloomsbury, 2014), the memoir *Sick* (HarperCollins, 2018), and the essay collection *Brown Album: Essays on Exile and Identity* (Vintage Books, 2020). Her nonfiction has appeared in many sections of the *New York Times*, *Los Angeles Times*, the *Washington Post*, *Elle*, *Slate*, *Salon*, and *Bookforum*, among many other publications. She has taught creative writing and literature at Johns Hopkins University, Wesleyan University, Columbia University, Bucknell University, Bard College, Sarah Lawrence College, and many other institutions around the country.

NIKITA LALWANI is an award-winning British novelist whose work has been translated into sixteen languages. Her first novel, *Gifted*, was longlisted for the Man Booker Prize, shortlisted for the Costa First Novel Award, and won the inaugural Desmond Elliott Prize. Her second, *The Village*, won a Jerwood Fiction Uncovered Prize.

TAEHUN LEE is a student at Duke University, majoring in evolutionary anthropology and minoring in education and medical sociology. He loves working with children and hopes for a better future, which is what led him to intern with the Korean Kids and Orphanage Outreach Mission. Taehun plans to work in the medical field in order to bring hope and smiles to many families.

KEVIN MOFFETT is the author of two story collections, a narrative app for mobile devices, and a pair of scripted podcasts, most recently *The Last Chapters of Richard Brown Winters*, forthcoming in 2021 from Gimlet Media.

LARISSA PHAM is an artist and writer in New York. She is the author of an essay collection, *Pop Song: Adventures in Art and Intimacy*, forthcoming in May 2021, and *Fantasian*, a novella. Her work has appeared in the *Paris Review Daily*, *Guernica*, the *Nation*, the *Believer*, and elsewhere.

LEGNA RODRÍGUEZ IGLESIAS was born in 1984 in Camagüey, Cuba, and now lives in Miami. She has won a number of major Cuban prizes, including the Premio Iberoamericano de Cuento Julio Cortázar, the Premio Calendario de Cuento, the Premio Calendario de Poesía, and the Premio Casa de las Américas de Teatro for her first play. She has published eleven books of poetry, three books of stories, two novels, and four children's books. The vast majority have never left the island, where her rising star has been called "El tsunami Legna."

MIKKEL ROSENGAARD is a Danish writer and the author of *The Invention of Ana* (HarperCollins, 2018). His writing has been published in five languages and has appeared in *Bookforum*, *BOMB*, and *Guernica*, on PBS's *Art21*, and elsewhere. He was born in Elsinore, Denmark, and lives in New York City.

SONDRA SILVERSTON is a native New Yorker who has been living in Israel for many years. Among her published translations are works by Israeli authors Amos Oz (*Between Friends* won the 2013 National Jewish Book Award for fiction), Eshkol Nevo (*Homesick* was won the 2009 Independent Foreign Fiction Prizelong list), Etgar Keret, Ayelet Gundar-Goshen (*Waking Lions* won the 2017 Jewish Quarterly Wingate Prize), Zeruya Shalev, Alona Frankel, and Savyon Liebrecht.

ESMÉ WEIJUN WANG is a novelist and essayist. She is the author of the *New York Times* best-selling essay collection *The Collected Schizophrenias* (2019), for which she won the Graywolf Press Nonfiction Prize, and a debut novel, *The Border of Paradise*, which was called a "Best Book of 2016" by NPR. She was named by *Granta* as one of the "Best of Young American Novelists" in 2017, and she won the Whiting Award in 2018. Born in the Midwest to Taiwanese parents, she lives in San Francisco, and can be found at esmewang.com and on Twitter at @esmewa.

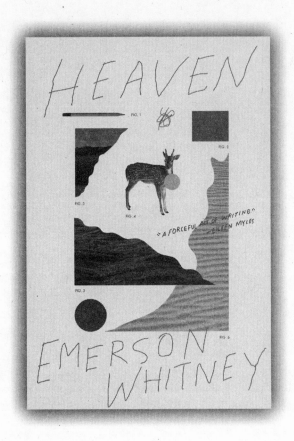

"*A poetic, candid, probing reckoning with childhood,
the maternal, gender, and the possibilities of theory, which
will both speak to its time and outlast it.*"
—Maggie Nelson

HEAVEN
by Emerson Whitney

An expansive examination of what makes us up, *Heaven* wonders what role
our childhood plays in who we are. Can we escape the discussion of causality?
Is the story of our body just ours? With extraordinary emotional force,
Whitney sways between theory and memory in order to explore these brazen
questions and write this unforgettable book.

ALSO AVAILABLE
FROM McSWEENEY'S

ART AND COMICS

BOOKS FOR CHILDREN

NONFICTION

HUMOR

POETRY

COLLINS LIBRARY

ALL THIS AND MORE AT

STORE.MCSWEENEYS.NET

Founded in 1998, McSweeney's is an independent publisher based in San Francisco. McSweeney's exists to champion ambitious and inspired new writing, and to challenge conventional expectations about where it's found, how it looks, and who participates. We're here to discover things we love, help them find their most resplendent form, and place them into the hands of curious, engaged readers.

THERE ARE SEVERAL WAYS TO SUPPORT MCSWEENEY'S:

Support Us on Patreon
visit *www.patreon.com/mcsweeneysinternettendency*

Subscribe & Shop
visit *store.mcsweeneys.net*

Volunteer & Intern
email *eric@mcsweeneys.net*

Sponsor Books & *Quarterlies*
email *amanda@mcsweeneys.net*

To learn more, please visit *www.mcsweeneys.net/donate*
or contact Executive Director Amanda Uhle at
amanda@mcsweeneys.net or 415.642.5609.

McSweeney's Literary Arts Fund is a nonprofit
organization as described by IRS 501(c)(3).
Your support is invaluable to us.

What's next?

McSWEENEY'S 64
THE AUDIO ISSUE

A SPRAWLING EXPERIMENT IN
AUDIO-VISUAL STORYTELLING,
CREATED IN COLLABORATION
WITH RADIOTOPIA.

FEATURING

Jason Reynolds

Kate Soper

Catherine Lacey

Rion Amilcar Scott

Aliya Pabani

John Lee Clark

David Weinberg

Aimee Bender

Sharon Mashihi

Kali Fajardo-Anstine

and many others, including fiction writers, audio
producers, voice actors, composers, illustrators,
playwrights, and grandmothers, all packaged
in an 8" × 10" box containing books, booklets,
a poster, a newspaper, a toy catalog, a key chain,
an eight-foot-long illustrated scroll, and more.

Subscribe at *store.mcsweeneys.net*